Scholastic World Cultures

THE MIDDLE EAST

by Clare McHugh
and the Editors of Scholastic Inc.

Fourth Edition

Consultant

PHILIP K. HITTI, Ph.D.

Professor Emeritus,
Department of Near Eastern Studies,
Princeton University.

Readability Consultant

LAWRENCE B. CHARRY, Ed.D.

📖 SCHOLASTIC INC.

Titles in This Series
CANADA
CHINA
GREAT BRITAIN
THE INDIAN SUBCONTINENT
JAPAN
LATIN AMERICA
MEXICO
THE MIDDLE EAST
SOUTHEAST ASIA
THE SOVIET UNION AND EASTERN EUROPE
TROPICAL AND SOUTHERN AFRICA
WESTERN EUROPE

ISBN 0-590-34750-0

Copyright © 1987, 1981, 1976, 1972 by Scholastic Inc.
All rights reserved.
Published by Scholastic Inc.
Printed in the U.S.A.
12 11 10 9 8 7 6   9 1
                                                        23

Publisher: *Eleanor Angeles*
Editorial Director for WORLD CULTURES: *Carolyn Jackson*
Assistant Editor: *Elise Bauman*

Art Director and Designer: *Irmgard Lochner*
Art Assistant: *Wilhelmina Reyinga*
Photo Editor: *Elnora Bode*

COVER: A solitary Middle Easterner—overshadowed by the timeless beauty of the Dome of the Rock, a Moslem mosque built in Jerusalem 1,200 years ago.

THE
MIDDLE EAST

Table of Contents

PROLOGUE

ON
MIDDLE
GROUND

MUCH OF THE region known as the Middle East is dry desert. The huge Sahara Desert in north Africa touches several Middle Eastern nations. And there are other deserts scattered throughout the region. It seldom rains in desert lands. Yet when it does rain, it pours

— pelting down in torrents, turning dry gulleys into rivers of slimy mud.

Like weather conditions in the region, the sprawling lands of the Middle East can surprise you. The region occupies a lot of territory, and it takes in many peoples. There are people who speak Arabic, Turkish, Hebrew, and other languages. There are Christians, Jews, and millions and millions of Moslems. In short, there is as wide-ranging a group of peoples as you can find anywhere on the globe.

These peoples have rarely been at peace for any lengthy stretch of time. And their various struggles often make worldwide headlines. But there is more to life in the Middle East than stories which make headlines. And to understand the headlines, it is necessary to know the cultural backgrounds of the peoples.

Israel is a Jewish nation. Most of its people are Jews. In the rest of the Middle East, the majority of the people are Arabs of the Moslem faith.

Many Arabs are angry over the existence of Israel. Arabs have lived for almost 13 centuries on the land that has become the nation of Israel, and many resent the Jews as intruders. On the other hand, for the last 2,000 years, Jews have looked upon Israel as the land to which they hoped they would return one day. Some Jews, indeed, have always lived on this land.

Since 1948 this dispute has caused a handful of wars — and uncountable small, but bloody, clashes. It has further divided a region already divided in several different ways. And it has shown again and again that what happens in the troubled Middle East will affect most nations of the world.

One thing that unites the many people of the area is the name we give them — "Middle Easterners." But what's "Middle" or "Eastern" about the nations of the

Middle East? After all, those countries are either on the northern edge of Africa or the western edge of Asia.

Part of the confusion lies in the fact that the term was invented by Europeans. They used the word "East" to distinguish the region from the "West" — that is, Western Europe. The way Europeans explained it, there were two "Easts" — a "Far East" (otherwise known as East Asia) and a "Near East" (that part of the "East" which, for Europeans, was closer to home).

That all seemed very clear to Europeans.

Unfortunately, it was anything but clear to the so-called "Near Easterners" themselves. To some of them it seemed as absurd to call themselves "Near Easterners" as it would to call Greeks "Near Westerners" or English "Far Westerners." And so, to clarify the name-calling — somewhat — the term *Middle East* was introduced.

The term has generally stuck. And actually it does make some sense. For the "Middle East" is indeed "middle" in one important way: it is a middle ground, linking the continents of Europe, Asia, and Africa and major bodies of water such as the Indian Ocean and the Mediterranean Sea.

Today the Middle East is swept up in a rolling tide of change that seems to threaten to split it apart. Some people struggle to achieve a more modern, Western way of life. Others, especially devout Moslems, seem to resent the effects of modernization. They seek to revive ancient religious and cultural traditions.

These changes make big differences in the way people think and act, the way they work and dress, even the way they look at one another. These differences, in turn, promise to create new challenges for the entire Middle East in the years ahead.

1
THE ARAB WAY

Chapter 1

The Land

IF THE WEATHER'S CLEAR, you can see the land and water from the cabin of a jet airplane 30,000 feet up.

You've left Rome or Athens headed east toward a land that has lured travelers for centuries. You skip across the island-dotted Aegean Sea, streaked with silver in the morning sun, and soon the saw-toothed coast of Turkey rises up before you. Your encounter with the Middle East has begun.

You fly east over the high, wide plateau of central Turkey with mountain ranges on your left and right. Now you're over a jumble of craggy ridges, where villages hang like eagles' nests from the mountainsides and shepherds herd their flocks in lonesome valleys. Up ahead tower the twin volcanoes of western Asia's tallest peak, Mount Ararat,* supposed port of call for Noah and his famous ark.

*See Pronunciation Guide.

Before you know it, you're over Iran. Below you lies the nation's breadbasket, a dry but fertile plateau dotted with wheat fields and fruit orchards. Your plane makes a right turn and you're in Iraq — over a V-shaped plain formed by two of the world's most historic rivers, the Tigris* and the Euphrates.* From your bird's-eye perch there seems nothing special about this plain — a fairly ordinary patchwork of farms and orchards and barren, open land. Yet it was here, more than 50 centuries ago, that restless people made the desert bloom and became the first to tell the tale in writing.

To the west yawns mile upon mile of empty desert. Political borders come up faster now — Jordan, a narrow slice of Syria, then Jordan again, and Israel. In the distance, up ahead of you, is the Mediterranean Sea, and along the coast stretches a narrow ribbon of farmland dotted every few miles with cities, towns, and villages. Below you lie the Holy Lands where two of the world's great religions — first Judaism, then Christianity — were born and a third, Islam, won many followers.

Next it's on across the Sinai* Peninsula, a triangle of desert land which links the continents of Asia and Africa. Then you come to the silent waters of the Suez Canal, a route used by some of the oil tankers as they make their way between the oil fields of the Arabian Peninsula and the shipping lanes of the Mediterranean Sea. Although you're now over Africa, the scenery remains much the same. All you can see is a blur of desert scrub and dry, rocky soil.

You'll be refueling in Cairo,* capital of the Arab Republic of Egypt, so you begin to descend. Approaching the city, your plane tilts its wings, allowing you a closer look at the world's longest river, the Nile. Here, 100 miles south of the Mediterranean, the

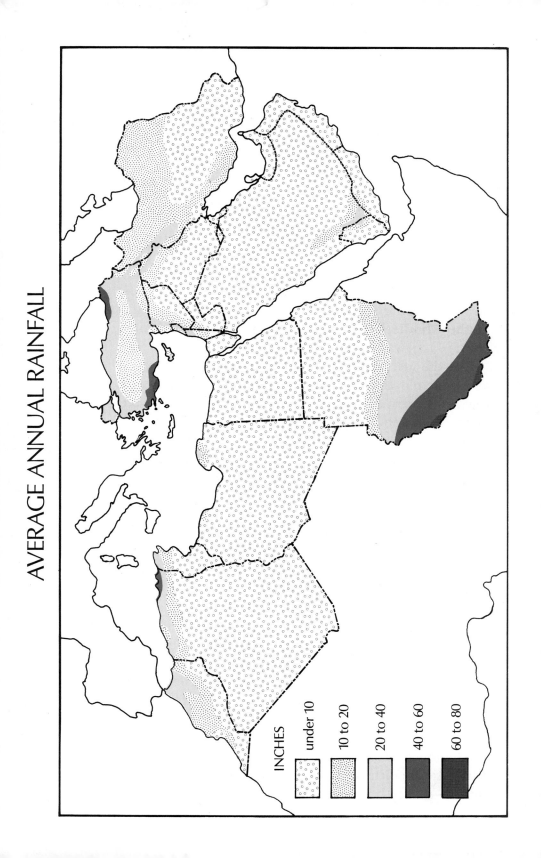

AVERAGE ANNUAL RAINFALL

INCHES

under 10

10 to 20

20 to 40

40 to 60

60 to 80

river is laced with bridges. Its banks are lined with boulevards. Much farther south — farther than the eye can see — lie the low, green river banks where Egyptian civilization dawned in the mists of the prehistoric past.

A dip of the wing flaps, a bump from the landing gear, and you're racing down a dusty runway at Cairo International Airport. Cairo is an ancient city, full of old stone houses and narrow, winding streets. It's also a booming metropolis — the most populous city of the Middle East and of the entire African continent.

But the last lap of your journey still beckons you, and your plane takes off again to rush you westward toward the setting sun. As you make your ascent, you approach an enormous limestone tableland called the Libyan Plateau. This tableland is one of the driest parts of the dusty Sahara — in fact, it is one of the driest parts of the earth's entire crust. In some parts it rains no more than once every 10 or 20 years.

Your jet flies on for hours across this gigantic sea of rock and sand, miles of it almost as desolate as the surface of the moon. Only now and then is the barrenness broken by splotches of green where palm trees mark the edge of an oasis.*

By now the sun is dipping low in the sky, shooting strands of light through snow-covered ridges on the far horizon. These mottled peaks are part of the Atlas Mountains, which march across North Africa from the northeastern tip of Tunisia to the southern edge of Morocco's Atlantic coast. On the far side of the Atlas is your destination: the twinkling lights of Casablanca on the Atlantic Ocean.

By now you've made a one-day sweep over most of the Middle East. You've covered nearly 6,000 miles — more than twice the air distance from New

LAND USE

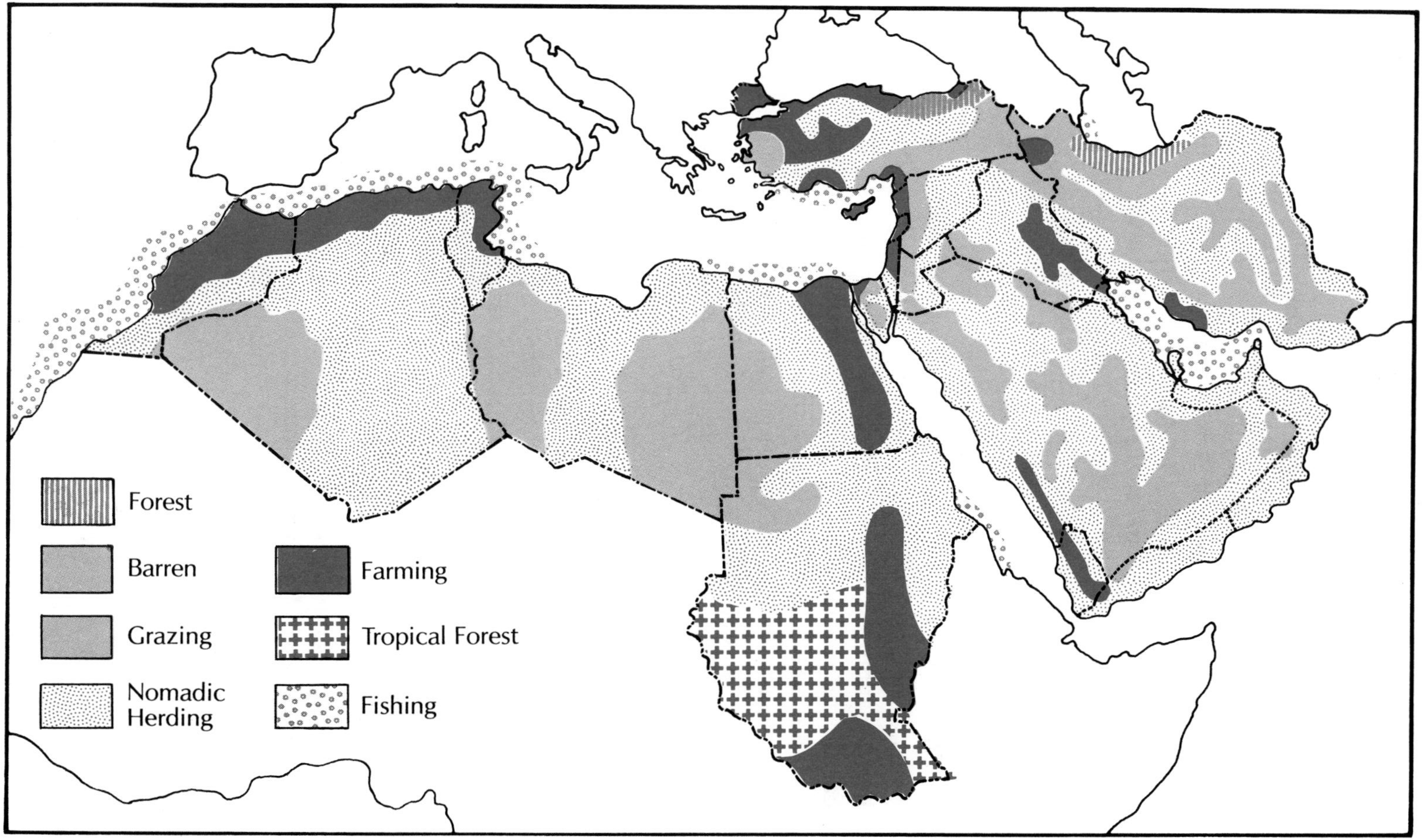

Forest

Barren

Grazing

Nomadic Herding

Farming

Tropical Forest

Fishing

York to San Francisco. You've flown over three continents — Europe, Asia, and Africa. You've flown over lands that border on three major bodies of water — the Mediterranean Sea, the Arabian Sea, and the Atlantic Ocean. You've had a bird's eye view of a region that is a major historical crossroads of our planet.

Most of the connecting links of this crossroads have surprisingly similar features. Basically those features can be placed in five main categories:

The Northern Tier (western Turkey and northern Iran). The most important feature of this region is its heavily mountainous terrain. The region's farming is carried on within two high central plateaus wedged into the mountains. The area's sharp-edged peaks not only look menacing, they sometimes actually move. In recent years, Turkey and Iran have been hit with several major earthquakes, which have taken many lives.

The Fertile Crescent (parts of Iran, Iraq, Syria, Lebanon, Jordan, and Israel). This region gets its name from its crescent shape on a map of the Middle East. Its reputation as fertile farmland dates back to Biblical times, and many scholars believe it was the site of the Garden of Eden. Despite its reputation, farming here is no easy job. Rains come mostly during the winter months and summers are very dry. Year after year peasants have tilled and watered and coaxed crops out of the land.

The Arabian Peninsula (Saudi Arabia, Yemen and South Yemen, Bahrain, Qatar, Oman, Kuwait, the United Arab Emirates). This boot-shaped peninsula is basically a giant hunk of sand-covered rock which peaks in the west and then tilts its way downward to the Persian Gulf. As real estate goes, it's more valuable for the oil which lies beneath its surface than for what little grows above ground. Though moun-

POPULATION DISTRIBUTION

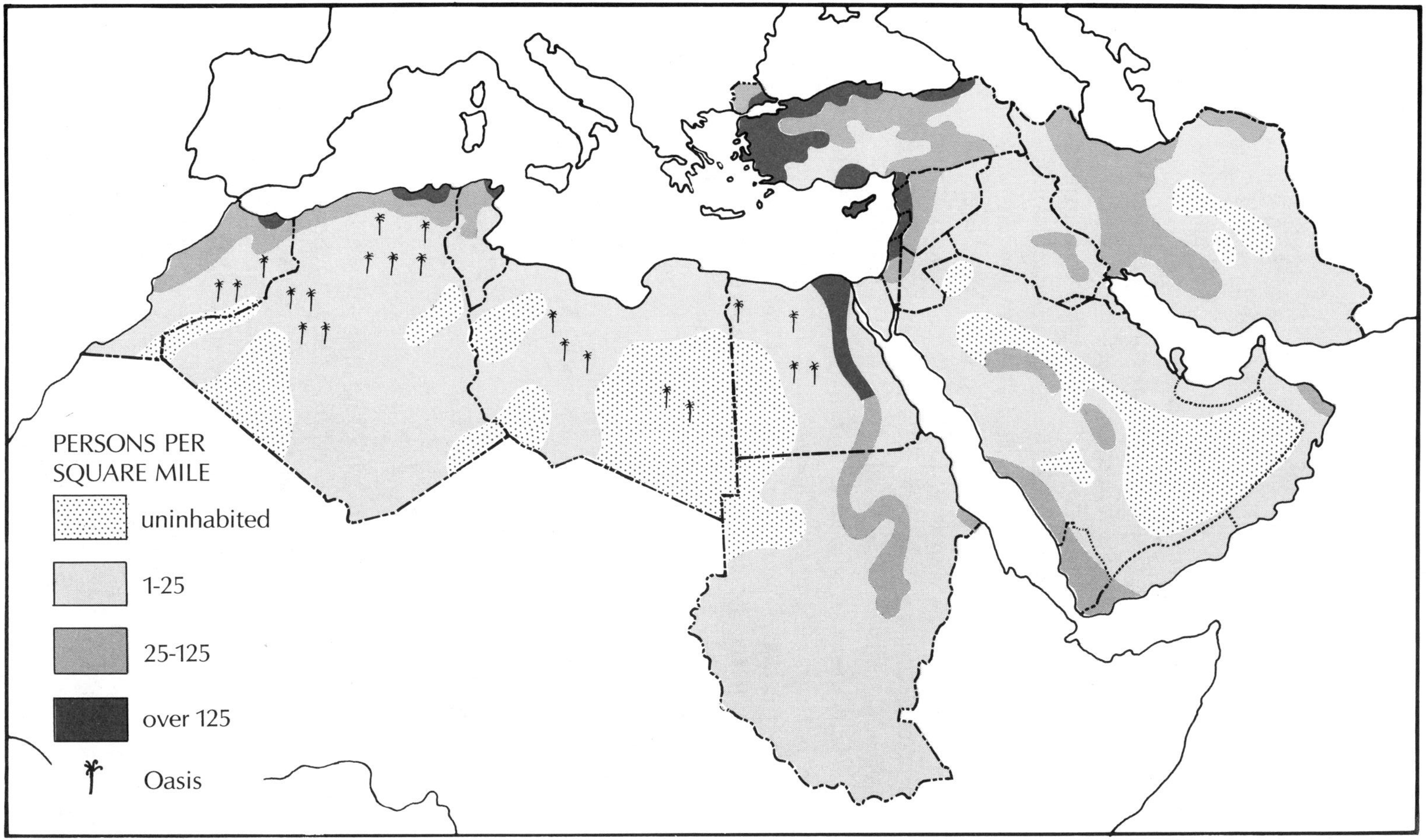

PERSONS PER
SQUARE MILE

uninhabited

1-25

25-125

over 125

Oasis

tains exist, most of the land is parched and barren desert. Much of it is unsettled, used only by wandering tribesmen and by very few of those.

The Nile River Basin (east-central Egypt and the Sudan). The Nile is the longest river in the world. It flows out of central Africa, and tumbles around mountains and through jungles and deserts for more than 4,000 miles. As it snakes its way downstream past the southern border of Egypt, it grows more and more vital to the people who live along its banks. For centuries, the waters of the Nile have irrigated a thin sliver of land on both banks.

The Sahara (Egypt, Libya, northern Sudan, southern parts of Tunisia, Algeria, and Morocco). This tawny no-man's-land ranks as the largest desert in the world. Its 3.3 million square miles nearly equal the area of the U.S. Contrary to the impression frequently given in movies and television shows, the Sahara is not all shifting, wind-blown sand dunes. It also contains vast mountain ranges and a plateau covered with bony, bare formations of rock. Whatever it's made of, this desert is big — and growing bigger. Experts tell us it's advancing southward at an average of 150 feet each year.

☆ ☆ ☆ ☆ ☆ ☆ ☆ ☆ ☆

These, then, are the main geographical features of the Middle East — generally flat, generally hot, generally dry. If most lands of the region share any one distinctive feature, it is their lack of rainfall. Only about five per cent of the total land area of the Middle East receives enough water for cultivation. And experts believe that only another five per cent could be made farmable with increased irrigation.

Lack of rainfall makes life hard for farmers, who make up a majority of Middle Easterners. It also poses problems for most Middle Eastern nations. With so little water to irrigate the land, few of these nations manage to grow enough food to feed themselves. Most do the best they can with what little fertile land they have. But all of them must import some food from abroad.

And so the physical setting of the Middle East directly affects the way its people get their food. It also affects much more than that. It influences the way they live and work. It has helped to mold their traditions over many years. And nowadays it shapes the way Middle Easterners react to the vast changes which are sweeping across their world.

Sumerian cuneiform, etched on wet clay and baked in the sun, is believed to be the world's oldest writing system.

WHERE HISTORY BEGAN

TIME CAN PLAY peculiar tricks on people, but have you ever heard of people playing tricks on time?

What if we were to turn the clocks of time back 50 or 60 centuries — to whirl ourselves back to the dawn of history? If we happened to land in the Middle East, we might get a close-up look at the people who first wrote about their comings and goings — who, in fact, first wrote. Period.

They were a people called Sumerians.* Our knowledge of the origins of the Sumerians is skimpy, to say the least. One scholarly hunch has it that these people were originally tribesmen who roamed inland from the Persian Gulf, never knowing where their next oasis was coming from. Some time before 4000 B.C. the Sumerians reached the plain between the Tigris and Euphrates rivers and found other peoples had already settled there. After the stark emptiness of the desert, the greenery of the plain looked inviting, so the Sumerians evidently decided to stop their wandering and settle down.

Slowly the Sumerians nursed this land into a gardening spot, then made the land their home. As they did so, they laid the foundations of their civilization. They taught themselves how to tell time in 60-minute hours and 24-hour days. They applied heat to metal to turn out a wide variety of tools and implements from cooking pots to plows. They used sails to harness the wind on water, thereby getting around the need to row their boats everywhere they went.

But their most remarkable achievement was writing, and they are believed to have been the first people to do it. They developed a "writing system" of 500 wedge-shaped characters known as cuneiform.* They drew these characters on wet clay tablets, then baked the tablets until they were dry. On the tablets the Sumerians spun stories and recorded business deals. Most important, they left behind a written record of their civilization — a record which goes by the name of history.

But the Sumerians were not the only people of their time who were accomplishing great things. Eight hundred miles to the southwest, along the fertile banks of the Nile River, the ancient Egyptians were building a civilization all their own. Like the Sumerians, the Egyptians were mainly a farming people. But unlike the Sumerians, who had formed a number of independent towns, the Egyptians went beyond the local level and organized a central government.

This organization was the work of a farsighted ruler named Menes,* who united the Nile Valley nations in about 3100 B.C. Menes is now thought to have been the first Egyptian *pharaoh** (or king). He and most of the pharaohs who followed him ruled with absolute power. They were backed by a class of nobles who enforced the laws and collected the taxes. The power of the pharaohs stemmed in part from the fact that the Egyptians worshiped them as gods.

The Egyptians believed in life after death. They thought the spirit of a dead pharaoh went to paradise, but now and then returned to inhabit his body. To allow the pharaohs to keep their privileged role after death, the Egyptians preserved their bodies by embalming them as mummies. At first they placed these mummies in simple tombs, but as the centuries passed these tombs grew steadily more elaborate. Finally this custom resulted in one of the most amazing construction jobs of all time — the building of the fabled Egyptian pyramids. Several of these pyramids still stand today near the banks of the Nile.

The pyramids have long outlived the civilization which created them. In fact, both Egypt and Sumer collapsed before invading armies.

All of this happened a long, long time ago. And yet time can play its peculiar tricks. Many who have studied the matter estimate that man has existed on Planet Earth some 1,000 or more centuries. The Sumerians and the Egyptians carved out their civilizations only a little more than 50 or 60 centuries ago. So, viewed against the timetable of human life, ancient history seems — well, almost modern.

THE RED SEA REGION

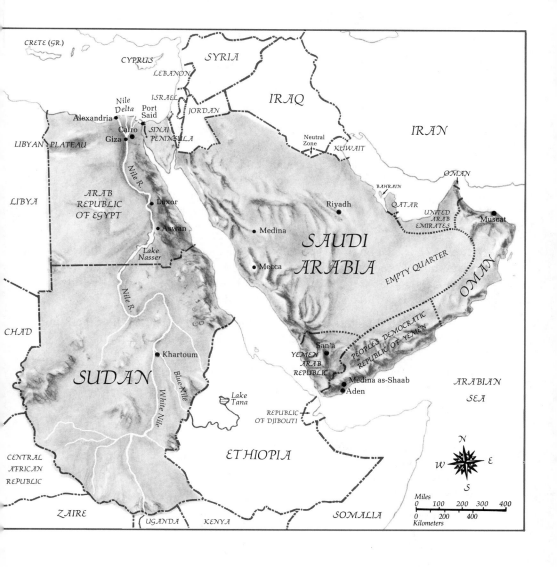

CRETE (GR.)

CYPRUS

SYRIA

LEBANON

ISRAEL

JORDAN

IRAQ

IRAN

Neutral Zone

KUWAIT

OMAN

BAHRAIN

QATAR

Nile Delta

Port Said

Alexandria

Cairo

Giza

SINAI PENINSULA

LIBYAN PLATEAU

LIBYA

ARAB REPUBLIC OF EGYPT

Nile R.

Luxor

Aswan

Lake Nasser

Riyadh

Medina

Mecca

SAUDI ARABIA

EMPTY QUARTER

UNITED ARAB EMIRATES

Muscat

OMAN

CHAD

Nile R.

Khartoum

SUDAN

Blue Nile

White Nile

Lake Tana

San'a

YEMEN ARAB REPUBLIC

PEOPLES DEMOCRATIC REPUBLIC OF YEMEN

Medina as-Shaab

Aden

ARABIAN SEA

CENTRAL AFRICAN REPUBLIC

REPUBLIC OF DJIBOUTI

ETHIOPIA

ZAIRE

UGANDA

KENYA

SOMALIA

N

W   E

S

Miles
0   100   200   300   400

0   200   400
Kilometers

Double-check

Review

1. What is the Sinai Peninsula?

2. What is the longest river in the world?

3. In which countries does the Fertile Crescent lie?

4. What was the Sumerians' most remarkable achievement?

5. Who is thought to have been the first Egyptian pharaoh?

Discussion

1. This chapter points out that land and climate help "shape the lives" of people in the Middle East. Think of the ways this is true for *your* community. Then compare your community with the information about the Middle East. Would it make sense to say, "Geography is destiny"? Why, or why not?

2. The construction of the pyramids in ancient Egypt required the work of thousands of laborers, perhaps slaves or volunteers. How do you think the pharaohs got laborers to do the work? How could people in the United States today be persuaded to work on this type of project?

3. What cultural factors might make one society — such as the Sumerian or the ancient Egyptian — more inventive and creative than another? Should a culture that is highly inventive or that has highly developed technology be thought of as "superior" to others? Why, or why not? What other things might indicate the "superiority" of a culture?

Activities

1. Some students might prepare a large wall map of the Middle East for use with this and future chapters. They could use the map on page 13 as a guide. From other maps, including maps in this book, add the names of the countries and other information to this wall map.

2. Ten words in Chapter 1 are starred (*). This indicates that they are in the Pronunciation Guide at the back of the book. A committee of students could assume primary responsibility for teaching fellow students how to pronounce these words. They could do this in advance for all future chapters.

3. The photo essays near the center of this book contain several photos showing the diversity of land in the Middle East. You might look at these photos now and mark on a map the places they show.

Skills

Use the maps "Average Annual Rainfall" and "Land Use" and information in Chapter 1 to answer the following questions.

1. Barren areas are marked by what color or design?
(a) dots   (b) gray   (c) dark blue

2. What do the numbers at the bottom left corner of the "Average Annual Rainfall" map indicate?
(a) average days of rainfall each year
(b) average amount in inches of heaviest rainfall each year
(c) average amount in inches of rainfall each year

3. Which of the following amounts of annual rainfall is most common in the Middle East?
(a) under 10 inches   (b) 10 to 20 inches   (c) 60 to 80 inches

4. Which of the following uses of land is least common in the Middle East?
(a) nomadic herding   (b) barren land   (c) forest

5. Judging from its name and its reputation, as described in Chapter 1, which of the following colors or designs is used to mark land use of at least part of the Fertile Crescent?
(a)gray   (b) dark blue   (c) blue dots

Chapter 2

Tradition and Change

FOR MORE THAN a thousand years, most of the people of the Middle East have called themselves Arabs. They mean by this that they speak the Arabic language and live the Arab way of life. This way of life is much the same from Morocco, on the west coast of Africa, to Oman, almost 4,000 miles east, on the shores of the Arabian Sea. So vast is the Arab world that it's easier to list the Middle Eastern countries which it *doesn't* include than to list the countries which it does.

The Arab world doesn't include Turkey and Iran, for most people from those countries speak Turkish, Persian, or Kurdish. Nor does it include Israel, for the dominant language there is Hebrew, and the way of life of many Israelis is closer to that of Europe and the U.S. than to the Arab world. But the Arab world *does* include most countries of the Fertile Crescent, the Arabian Peninsula, and North Africa. And these countries contain a majority of the people of the Middle East.

Like many other peoples around the globe, the Arabs place great emphasis on their traditions. Probably the most important influence on those traditions is religion. Though some Arabs are Christians or Jews, by far the largest number are Moslems. They govern their lives according to the laws of their religion, Islam, as do most Turks and Iranians.

This religion arises from the teachings of an Arab named Mohammed, who lived in the seventh century A.D. (see page 34). Like Abraham, Moses, and Jesus before him, Mohammed stressed belief in one Supreme Being. Moslems call their God Allah. They believe that the words of Allah, as heard by Mohammed, were written down in a holy book called the Koran.*

One passage from the Koran describes how the faithful look upon Allah. *"He is God, the One and Only; God, the Eternal, Absolute."*

Moslems believe that Allah is responsible for the differences which exist between people on earth — the differences, say, between rich and poor. Says the Koran: *"We have created you in degrees, one above the other."*

Since these differences are all of Allah's making, Moslems believe that virtuous people must accept them honorably. For the most part, Moslems are taught to accept their lot in life as fate.

According to the Koran, a man may have as many as four wives at one time. Four wives are therefore legal in most Moslem countries. The Koran also says that *"men are the managers of the affairs of women."* A number of Moslem customs are based on this rule, and in many areas they are strictly followed.

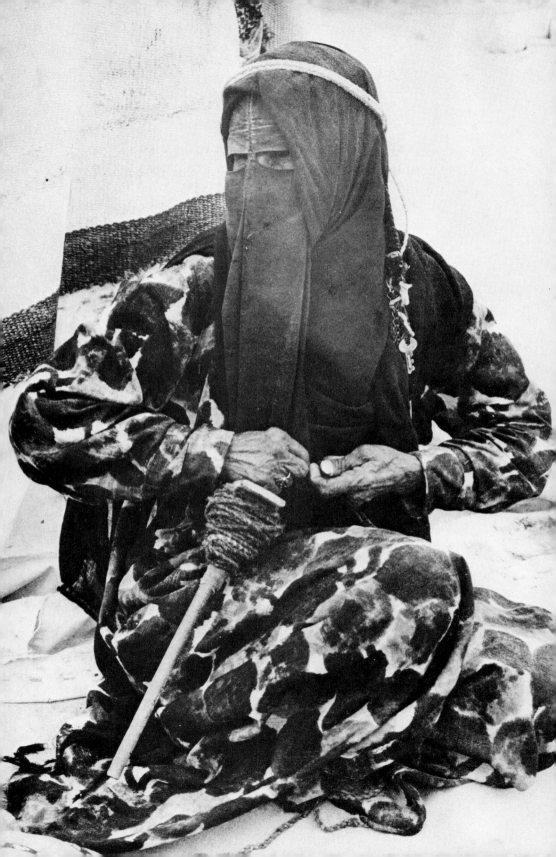

For example, in many Middle Eastern countries, the women are expected to lead secluded lives. In a traditional Moslem home, a separate area, called a *harem*,* is set aside for them. Only men who are members of the family may enter it. Outside their homes women cover their faces with veils. They avoid strangers and never go to public places such as restaurants.

Many Middle Easterners also think it is wrong for girls to attend school. Since Moslem women are supposed to spend most of their time at home, these people believe the women do not need an education.

Other Moslem traditions are also closely observed in parts of many Middle Eastern countries. Since the Koran forbids alcoholic drinks, no wine or liquor may be sold publicly in Saudi Arabia, Yemen, Kuwait, or Iran. Traditional Moslem rules forbid the showing of people or animals in paintings or sculpture. These rules aren't always observed, but Saudi Arabia and Iran prohibit movie theaters. This prohibition may have as much to do with keeping out foreign influence as with observing Moslem traditions strictly.

Not all Moslems interpret the laws of Islam strictly. Most Moslem countries allow the sale of wine and liquor, though most devout Moslems refuse it. Outside Saudi Arabia and Iran, movies are available and highly popular in the Middle East. And many Moslem artists no longer feel bound by the rule against portraying human beings in their art.

Still, the traditions of Islam continue to exercise a strong influence on Arab traditions. So, too, does the

A veiled Bedouin women spins wool by her tent. The tent, which she spun and wove herself, gives her family shelter from the harsh Saudi Arabian desert.

Arabic language, which serves as the "mother tongue" for more than 100 million people. For many Arabs, their language has a special significance, beyond the basic idea of conveying ideas and information.

Actually there are two Arabics. One is the written language which, as you can see below, is written in a graceful, flowing script. The other is the spoken language, which comes in several different dialects depending on the area of the Arab world. Spoken Arabic bears little resemblance to the formal, written style. Many Arabs greatly revere the spoken language, as this old Arab proverb indicates:

"Wisdom has alighted on three things: the brain of the Franks, the hands of the Chinese, and the tongue of the Arabs."

The importance placed on spoken Arabic shows up in the attention Arabs have paid to oral poetry. A century before Mohammed, Arab tribesmen listened in rapt silence while poets recited at fairs and other public gatherings. Long after Mohammed's death, poets continued to serve as speakers for their tribes, extolling virtues such as honesty and generosity and molding public opinion in many ways.

Arabic script reads "Kingdom of Saudi Arabia."

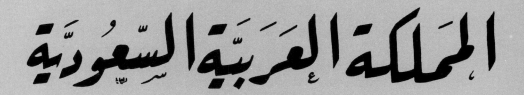

Arab poets were particularly adept at describing their desert surroundings. But their most important task was inspiring other members of their tribes to deeds of daring or good will.

Here is how one of them, a sixth-century poet named Salamah,* described tribal life in a poem entitled "Gone Is Youth":

When wind blows chill from the North, we pitch our tents in the dales where drought has left . . . stumps and brushes to burn. . . .
When one comes calling to us for help, . . . clear is our answer to him — forth start we straight in his cause;
Swiftly we saddle the camels strong and eager to go, and quick we set on our short-haired steeds the gear for the road.

Though the great age of Arab poetry is a thing of the past, Arab reverence for the spoken language has lingered into the present. Even today, for example, Arabs attach great value to the ability to chant long sections of the Koran from memory. They enjoy listening to popular Arabic songs. In night clubs and concert halls from Cairo to Casablanca, Arab singers belt out ballads which speak directly to the soul.

Language — spoken, sung, or chanted — thus serves as a major force uniting the Arab world. Arab architecture gives this world a style all its own. In part, Arab building is an outgrowth of the Islamic faith. As builders, the Arabs have presented the world with two lasting religious features — the *mosque** and the *minaret.**

Mosques (or Moslem houses of worship) stand at the center of nearly every village, town, and city across the Arab world. Most are rectangular buildings

Arab husband leads his two wives down a city street.

with large, open courtyards in the center. At one or two outside corners of the mosque are minarets — towerlike structures. Some minarets are thin and straight, like pencils, while others curve upward in spiral shapes. In cities, towns, and villages, towers of the minarets perform a specific religious purpose. They are used five times a day by a Moslem official called a *muezzin,** when he summons the people to prayer. Recently, in many Arab cities, a recording has replaced the muezzin.

In town after town in the Middle East, the elegance of the town's mosque contrasts vividly with its harsh desert backdrop. In larger Arab cities the flowing lines of these buildings contrast even more sharply with the straight, sharp shape of modern buildings perhaps right down the block. The mosques are a sign of Arab devotion to tradition. But the modern buildings are a sign that things are changing, too.

Tradition and change. These will be two of the main themes of this book. Tall buildings rise over the cities of the Arab world. New irrigation projects come to the villages. Even in the parched deserts, oil wells sprout where once only camels and goats grazed.

But even as things change, certain traditions remain strong. The people of the Arab world retain a strong love for their old values: for their families, for the active life, for the spoken word, and — most important — for the teachings of Islam.

Thousands of devout Muslim pilgrims gather for midday prayers outside the sacred mosque in Mecca.

PROPHET TO MILLIONS

"There is no God but Allah, and Mohammed is His Messenger."

THESE WORDS serve as the basic creed for more than 550 million Moslems around the world today. Like Jews and Christians, Moslems believe in one Supreme Being. Moslems call this being Allah. But who was Mohammed, the prophet of so popular a faith?

His story begins in the latter half of the sixth century A.D. in the city of Mecca near the western coast of the

Arabian Peninsula. Once merely an outpost for wandering tribes, Mecca had recently blossomed into a prosperous way-station on the trading route from Syria to Yemen. Though trade made many Meccans very wealthy, it also troubled many others. By promoting trade, some believed, their city was winning wealth and power at the expense of older values such as honesty, generosity, and honor.

It was into this world of doubt that Mohammed was born about 570 A.D. He was the son of a not-very-well-to-do Meccan from the city's leading tribe. During his early manhood, Mohammed met a wealthy widow named Khadija.* He agreed to enter her employ, probably to help her manage her business affairs. At the age of about 25, he married her. Throughout the early years of the marriage, the couple is believed to have led a quiet, peaceful life.

As far as historians know, Mohammed observed at least some of the usual religious customs of his day. Those customs included belief in a number of pagan gods, a variety of superstitions, and several sorts of idols. But these beliefs disturbed Mohammed. When he was troubled, he would follow an age-old Arab practice and retreat to an isolated spot outside the city to meditate.

While he was meditating one night in 610 A.D., a strange thing happened. Mohammed heard a voice which ordered him: "Recite in the name of the Lord!" At first he was filled with terror, but in the following days and months he kept on hearing the voice. Under the steady encouragement of his wife, Khadija, he persuaded himself to begin preaching.

His sermon was simple: There was only one God, Allah, and he, Mohammed, was God's Messenger on earth.

Mohammed preached that Allah had unlimited power on earth and in heaven and that he would judge all creatures. But this God of justice was also a God of mercy. Through prayer, faith, and charity, people can repent and purify themselves, and attain Paradise after death.

He called his teachings Islam, meaning "submission to God's will." His first convert was Khadija, and other converts soon followed. Most were young people, rebels against Mecca's worship of wealth and power. By joining the Moslem movement, they hoped to return to older values such as generosity and honor.

As converts to Islam increased, so did opposition to it from the rulers of Mecca. These rulers received much of their income from pagan pilgrimages to their city. So, quite naturally, they supported the worship of the pagan gods.

Townspeople laughed at the Moslems, insulted them, scorned them. They even heaped garbage at the doors of Moslem homes. Soon, persecution was running rampant in Mecca. Then another blow hit Mohammed. Khadija fell ill and died.

Judging from the abuse he was receiving in Mecca, Mohammed decided he had won nearly all the converts he was going to win there for the time being. In 622 A.D. he and his followers packed their belongings, bade farewell to their families, and fled on a journey into unknown territory. Their destination was a northern oasis today known as Medina.*

This journey proved to be the crucial turning point in the history of Islam. Moslems now call this flight the *hegira,** or migration. They mark the year it took place — 622 — as the start of their calendar, just as Christians mark the birth date of Jesus as the start of theirs.

Unlike Mecca, Medina proved to be fertile soil for the growing faith. Islam quickly attracted a wide following, and Mohammed almost immediately became the leader of the entire community.

During the next few years Mohammed steadily gained the confidence of his new community. As he did so, he followed the usual Arab custom of taking several wives at once.

Mohammed proved himself an astute lawmaker, setting rules on matters ranging from inheritance to diet. He also proved himself expert at military affairs. Under his direction, the Moslem community staged a number of successful raids on passing caravans. One success led to another until the Moslems were ready to retake Mecca, which they still regarded as their spiritual home.

In 630 Moslem armies laid siege to the city. The Meccans were in no mood for fighting, and the city fell with little bloodshed.

Within the next two years, most of the Arabian Peninsula fell to Islam. Mohammed reigned as the undisputed religious leader of this desert world.

In 632 he fell ill and died. According to tradition, the news of his passing was made public by his closest friend. "If you are worshipers of Mohammed, know that he is dead," the friend is believed to have said. He added: "If you are worshipers of God, know that God is living and does not die."

It was a fitting farewell. For Mohammed had repeatedly stressed that he was God's *Messenger* and nothing more. Today Moslems sometimes wince when outsiders refer to their religion as "Mohammedanism," thereby seeming to place Mohammed in a divine role. To Moslems their prophet was simply a man who heard God's calling and spread it far and wide.

Double-check

Review

1. What areas does the Arab world include?

2. Why may alcoholic drinks not be sold publicly in Saudi Arabia?

3. When and why are minarets used?

4. What "sermon" did Mohammed preach?

5. What does *Islam* mean in English?

Discussion

1. The Arab world observes many traditions. To what extent are these traditions from before the time of Mohammed? To what extent are the traditions a result of the influence of Islam? Why do you suppose that Moslem traditions are observed more strictly in some parts of the Arab world than in other parts?

2. In Saudi Arabia, boys and girls attend separate schools. Male teachers cannot teach female students, except by closed-circuit television. Why do you suppose this is so? What are the advantages and disadvantages of such a system? Why do you think public schools in the United States are co-ed? What, if anything, does this difference suggest about different attitudes toward education in the two countries?

3. Do you agree with the Moslem belief that people should passively accept their lot in life? What people you know accept this idea? What people you know do *not* accept this idea? How might the second group of people be different if they did accept this idea?

Activities

1. Someone of the Moslem faith might be invited to speak to the class. Students could prepare questions to ask the speaker about the religious beliefs and practices of Islam on such subjects as prayer, gender roles, diet, and education.

2. Some students may wish to make drawings or models of a mosque, using examples found in an encyclopedia or a picture book. When finished, students could display the art projects in the classroom.

3. Several students might pretend to be early followers of Mohammed and write letters to their families in 622 A.D., telling them why they are fleeing Mecca and urging them, for reasons the students state in their letters, to convert to Islam.

Skills

March 1976–February 1977

Page 964   SAUDI ARABIA — *Continued*

Industries

Aladdin's troubled dream. J. Flanigan. il Forbes 117:28-32+
F 15 '76
Saudi slowdown hits U.S. builders. Bus W p35-6 S 20 '76
See also
Petroleum industry — Saudi Arabia
SAUDI ARABIAN pottery. See Pottery, Saudi Arabian
SAUDIA (airline) See Airlines — Saudi Arabia
SAUGUS, Mass.
   Don't bury garbage, generate tax revenues, B. Forestell. il Am
   City & County 91:51-4 My '76
SAUNA
   Some like it hot: steam bath vs sauna. C. Duhé. Am Home
   79:10+ N '76

Abbreviations	il — illustrated
F — February	+ — continued on later pages
My — May	Bus W — *Business Week*
N — November	Am Home — *American Home*
S — September	Am City & County — *American City & Country*

Use the above material from Readers' Guide to Periodical Literature *and information in Chapter 2 to answer the following questions.*

1. In which of the following publications will you find the articles listed in *Readers' Guide?*
(a) newspapers   (b) magazines   (c) books

2. How many articles are listed above?
(a) four   (b) five   (c) seven

3. How long a period of time is covered by this edition of *Readers' Guide?*
(a) one year   (b) two months   (c) two years

4. Under which letter of the alphabet would you look in *Readers' Guide* for listings of articles about Saudi Arabian pottery?
(a) A   (b) C   (c) P

5. In which magazines are articles which might relate to information in Chapter 2?

Chapter 3

Desert Dwellers

HASSAN* IS 16 years old. In those 16 years, he has slept under a solid roof only once or twice. His home has been a "house of hair" — a tent made of cloth woven from black goat's hair. He has never been to school, and he cannot read or write. But he can hunt, and he can ride a camel or a horse. He can find his way where there are no roads, trees, mountains, lakes, or rivers — in fact, where there are no landmarks of any kind. Alone in the wilderness except for his camel, he knows how to survive.

Hassan is a Bedouin* who lives by wandering from place to place. His home is a part of Saudi Arabia called the Empty Quarter. Mostly barren and forbidding, it is one of the largest deserts in the world.

Like all Bedouins, Hassan belongs to a tribe. He is a member of the Murrah* tribe, which probably

dates back before the time of Mohammed. Murrah tribesmen are camel-raisers who wander in the desert with their herds, never staying very long in one place. When they need a fresh supply of water or their camels need a greener pasture, they pack their belongings and change camp.

The Murrah is a large tribe of about 6,000 people. It is divided into many small groups of families who travel about with their herds. Each group of families is a *clan*. In Hassan's clan there are 25 families, all related to one another. All these families live in tents similar to Hassan's.

Hassan's mother, Amina,* wove the cloth for her family's house of hair. She also made the long curtain which divides the inside of the tent into two sections. One side is for the men; the other, for the women. On the men's side, Hassan's father, Abdullah,* entertains male guests who come to the tent. On the other side of the curtain is the harem, where Hassan's mother and his two sisters live.

In the evening — unless there are male guests — the family has its main meal together in the harem. Only men who are members of the family are permitted in the harem. If Abdullah has male guests, the men dine in their own part of the tent. The women never leave the harem if there are strangers in the men's part of the tent.

Summer months are dry in the desert, and tribesmen must stay close to the villages and the wells. In late October, the rains begin again, and the clan begins its travels. After the ground has been moistened by showers, patches of green sprout in the sand. All winter long the Bedouins and their herds follow these showers.

In winter the clan changes its camp about every 10 days. By that time the camels have usually eaten all the grass around the campsite, and the sheik,* the chief of the clan, guides his people to another site. He tries to find an area where rain has recently fallen and grass has just sprouted. As long as the camels have fresh grass to eat, they can go without water for several days — much longer than can human beings or other animals. However, about every fifth day or so, the camels will also need water to drink. Then the clan must be sure that they can get to a well or a stream.

The sheik often holds a meeting in his tent with the other older men of the clan to talk over the problem of finding water and grass. Any elder may offer advice or give his opinion, and the sheik will listen with attention. Arabs have great respect for older men and believe that age and experience bring wisdom and skill.

Hassan helps in many ways with the work of the clan, mostly by caring for the camels. Selling and trading camels is the clan's way of making a living. The camels also supply much of what the Bedouins need for their daily lives: milk to drink; hair to make the cloth for tents and clothing; and hides to make sandals, waterbags, and many other useful items. Sometimes camels also provide meat, although the Bedouins seldom kill such extremely valuable animals for food.

So far this year the rains have not been plentiful, and grass and water have been hard to find. There is talk in the clan that they may face a drought — a period of no rain at all — in the next few months. The sheik heard warnings of a drought on his transistor radio, the only one in camp. Until the sheik bought his radio, the Bedouins heard news of events outside the clan only when they visited the villages or met other tribesmen at the wells.

✑ If Abdullah has male guests, the men dine in their own part of the tent, while the women remain in the harem.

Often in the evening Abdullah visits the sheik's tent with the other clansmen. There they gather to relax and talk, and enjoy their favorite drink, coffee.

On this night, the sheik reports that a new grazing place has been found which should last the camels about two weeks. But the water nearby is brackish — fit for the animals, but too salty for human beings. This means that the clan will have only camel's and goat's milk to drink. No one is too bothered, for they have often gone without water before. The men linger over the coffee, drinking three cups each, and talking long into the night.

☆ ☆ ☆ ☆ ☆ ☆ ☆ ☆ ☆

During the rainless summer, Bedouin tribes live near the settlements. Members of different tribes meet, and the Bedouins visit their friends among the town-dwellers. Also during the summer months the Bedouins do most of their trading.

Early in the morning on market days Bedouins throng the roads leading to town. For trading they bring camels, sheep, goats, hides, wool, and the rugs and cloth made by the women.

In the village square where the market is held, the merchants arrange their wares on the ground and squat beside them. Tools, water jars, cooking utensils, daggers, medicines, candy, clothing, and many other items are on display.

Bedouin men (top right) relax over coffee. Bedouin women (bottom right) tend to children in their harem.

⩰ Faster and faster, Hassan's world is disappearing.

When a customer approaches, the seller does not name a price. Instead, the buyer makes an offer. The merchant, praising his wares highly, states a higher amount. This bargaining goes on and on until a price is finally agreed on and the trade is made. Arabs love to bargain and to be able to boast of how cheaply they bought a valuable item.

The most important event before the coming of the winter rains will be Hassan's wedding to Fatimah,* one of his many cousins. By the time the wedding takes place she will be 15. Bedouin girls usually do not marry much later than that.

Abdullah and Fatimah's father have already met to decide on what the marriage contract terms will be. One of these is the amount of the *mahr,** the gift which must be given by the groom to his bride. Hassan will pay his mahr in the form of animals — camels, sheep, and goats — which his father will give him.

The parents of Hassan and Fatimah were the ones who decided that the two young people should be married. Some brides never even see their future husbands until the day of the wedding. Many Arabs, especially Bedouins, still follow this custom. But many others, especially in the cities, have greater freedom to choose their own mates by themselves.

After the mahr has been paid, the wedding festivities will begin. There will be four separate celebrations. Not only will the families of the bride and groom celebrate separately, but the men and women of each family will have their own separate feasts.

When the male guests have assembled, the ser-

Workers at Arabian oil refinery head home at end of day.

vants will bring in trays of lamb stuffed with rice. Everyone will help himself from these dishes, dipping in with the fingers of his right hand (the left hand is considered unclean). Then the men will celebrate long into the night.

On the other side of the tent curtain, in the harem, Amina and all the women guests will also be feasting and celebrating. They will not join the men. According to Moslem custom, men and women do not mingle at such large gatherings.

The wedding celebrations in the tents of the two families may last as long as three days. Finally Hassan will take his bride home to his family's tent, and the wedding will be over. After his wedding, Hassan will have several camels and many sheep and goats of his own, presents from his family and Fatimah's. When the sheik calls a meeting of the men of the clan, Hassan will sit with them. As a married man, he will join the other men of his clan as an equal.

☆ ☆ ☆ ☆ ☆ ☆ ☆ ☆ ☆

Faster and faster, Hassan's world is disappearing. All over the Middle East, the number of wandering herdsmen grows smaller each year. New discoveries and developments, such as new sources of water and modern means of transportation, are changing the face of the desert itself.

Once camels were the only means of crossing the vast deserts of the Middle East. Now airplanes, helicopters, jeeps, and trucks are replacing the old camel caravans. Camels, no longer so vital to trade, no longer bring a high price in the markets. Except for the Bedouins, few people need them nowadays. Today sheep, which provide most of the meat eaten in Saudi Arabia, are more important in the marketplaces than camels. The day may soon come when a person cannot earn a living by raising and selling camels. Already many Bedouins are being forced to leave the desert and take up some other work.

In Saudi Arabia, one of the main reasons why the life of the Bedouins and all the other people is changing is oil. Although it was discovered in the Arabian Peninsula as recently as the 1930's, Saudi Arabia has since become one of the great oil-producing countries of the world. With a population of more than nine million, Saudi Arabia each year earns as much as 50 billion dollars from its oil (see Chapter 12).

Hassan may some day decide to give up the desert and work at one of the many new jobs in the oil industry. The area through which his tribe travels is close to the oil center of the country.

Some Bedouins have not been willing to give up their old life completely. But many have compromised. During the winter they pasture their animals on the desert. When the summer comes they move to the cities. Some members of the family may live near the city all year round.

Many Arabs whose families have lived for centuries in cities are proud to claim Bedouins as ancestors. The Bedouins' nomadic way of life seems destined to disappear, but it will certainly not be forgotten.

Double-check

Review

1. What is Hassan's tent made of?

2. Which is the driest season in the desert?

3. With what useful things do camels provide Bedouins?

4. What is a *mahr?*

5. What forms of transportation are replacing the old camel caravans in the desert?

Discussion

1. What would you miss most about your present life-style if you became a nomad? What would you enjoy most about being a nomad? In what ways, if you became a nomad, would your attitudes be changed toward the importance of family, education, land ownership, and government?

2. Hassan and Fatimah's marriage was arranged by their parents. What might be the advantages and drawbacks of this type of marriage? How successful do you think these arranged marriages are? Would you want your parents to pick a marriage partner for you? Explain your answers.

3. Middle Eastern countries such as Saudi Arabia are becoming modernized. More industries are being developed, and cities are growing larger. How might these developments affect the Bedouins' nomadic way of life? Their clan organizations? Their arranged marriages and other customs? Would the changes be for the better, or for the worse? Why?

Activities

1. Some students might look in magazines, newspapers, and other sources for pictures of Bedouins and the nomadic way of life on the desert. They could arrange a bulletin board display on the subject.

2. Some students might want to research one of the following aspects of the natural history of the desert: animals, birds, insects, plants, rainfall patterns, or soils. Students could give oral reports on their subjects to the rest of the class.

3. Several pairs of students could role-play a merchant and a customer in an Arab market. Use items in the classroom as the "merchandise" and spread them on the floor or on a desk. Then the "customer" and the "merchant" bargain until they agree on a price. Have the class vote on which student got the best deal.

Skills

THE WORLD'S LARGEST DESERTS

Name	Area (in thousands of square miles)	Location
Sahara	3,320	Northern Africa
Gobi	500	Mongolia and China
Rub al-Khali (Empty Quarter)	250	Arabia
Gibson	250	Western Australia
Great Victoria	250	Western and Southern Australia
Kalahari	225	Southern Africa

Source: The World Almanac

Use the table above and information in Chapter 3 to answer the following questions.

1. What does this table give information about?

2. Where did the information in this table come from?

3. How large is the Gobi Desert in area?

4. Which two deserts are located in Australia?

5. What is the Arabic name of the desert in which the Murrah tribe lives?

Chapter 4

Farmers of the Nile

IT IS A BRIGHT MORNING in a land where the sun shines steadily and summer seems to last all year. Along a road lined with palm trees, farmers walk to the fields. Because of the heat, the farmers are bare-chested and barefoot and wear only skirt-like garments which reach to their knees. On their shoulders they carry long-handled hoes made entirely of wood, even to the pointed tips.

Close to the road flows the longest river in the world, the Nile. All the water the people have comes from this river, for it rains here only two or three days a year. Without the Nile, there would be no water to drink, no water for the crops. Without the river, there would be little life.

This is Egypt, and the people are Egyptian farmers of the Nile valley.

Just beyond the village lie fields of wheat, melons, and vegetables. Beyond the fields lies the desert, the home of the Egyptian Bedouins. In the past, the Bedouins and the villagers were on less than friendly

*Mud-walled houses and shops cluster
together tightly along the narrow, twisting
streets of a village in the Nile River valley.*

terms, for the Bedouins used to make it a practice of raiding the village for food. So, for protection, village leaders long ago built a high wall around their settlement. The wall still stands, and inside it houses and shops are clustered together along narrow, winding streets.

In this village lives a 14-year-old girl named Fawzia.* Her father, Ahmed,* farms a plot of ground a little more than five acres in size. Since few villagers own much more than one acre of land, Fawzia's father is fairly well-to-do.

In Egypt, farmers are called *fellahin*,* the Arabic word for "those who plow the land." Like most fellahin, Ahmed and his family live in the village, not on the land they farm. Ahmed's house is one story high and has three rooms, built around a courtyard. The family of six lives in two of the rooms. The third serves as a kind of stable for the family's animals — a cow, a donkey, a water buffalo, and some chickens. Like most fellahin, Ahmed cannot afford a separate stable outside his house.

The house, like all the others, is made of mud brick. The floors are of beaten earth, pressed down until they are firm and level. The roof is flat, covered with palm boughs and straw. Except for the date palms which line the banks of the Nile, Egypt has few trees whose wood is hard enough to use for building. The date trees are too valuable to be cut down for wood. So from ancient times the people have built their homes of stone or of mud bricks mixed with straw and dried in the sun.

Life in the village begins each day with a prayer at dawn. In towns and villages, people are called to prayer by the muezzin, a man employed just for this purpose. Five times a day the muezzin climbs the stairs to the top of the minaret, the tower of the mosque, and calls out over the rooftops to the people. At dawn, his opening words include the reminder, "Prayer is better than sleep...."

Fawzia awakens each morning to this call. Everyone in the family — Fawzia; her parents; and her three brothers, Hashem,* 17, Hamid,* eight, and Fouad,* four — sleeps on cotton mattresses which are rolled up and stacked against the wall during the day. The room in which the family sleeps serves also as kitchen and dining room.

Fawzia's first task each morning is to milk the water buffalo. The members of her family always have fresh milk for breakfast, as well as tea and bread. Often they also have cheese and sometimes brown beans left to cook during the night. But the family does not eat the eggs their chickens lay; they save those to sell.

By the time the family finishes breakfast, the sun is well up and the village streets are crowded with people. Ahmed and Hashem trudge off to the fields. Hamid rushes off to school. And Fawzia goes to the village well. Many of the village girls will be doing the same, and she will meet most of her friends there.

With her water jar, Fawzia leaves the house, taking care to cover the lower part of her face with a veil of sheer black material. On her way to the well, Fawzia passes the road leading to the fields where Ahmed and Hashem are watering the land with a device known as a *shadoof*.* It consists of a long pole which swings up and down somewhat like a seesaw. A bucket, attached to one end of the pole, is pushed down into the water, then lifted and swung round — to tip its load into an irrigation ditch. To U.S. farmers this might seem a tedious way to water crops. But it works, and Egyptian farmers have used it for more than 3,000 years.

In fact, such devices are being used overtime these days, for farmers along the Nile generally do more planting than they used to. They are doing so largely because of dams built by the government in recent years. These dams store up much of the water from fall flooding, for irrigation use during the dry season. The biggest dam of all was completed in 1970 at Aswan,* a town in southern Egypt. Called the Aswan High Dam, it is one of the biggest in the world.

Before such dams were built, most Egyptian fellahin planted one crop a year — after the fall floods. Now that the dams provide water all year round, Ahmed and the men of his village now plant two crops. And in some parts of the country, the fellahin grow three crops a year.

After their long morning's work at the shadoof, Ahmed and Hashem are ready for an early lunch. Fawzia brings it to them in the fields at about 11 o'clock. After lunch, the men sleep through the early afternoon hours, the hottest part of the day. Then they work again until dusk.

Evenings are quiet in Fawzia's village. Supper is a hot meal, perhaps bean soup or stewed beans, or fish from the Nile. Every one or two months there may be some chicken or water buffalo, but most fellahin cannot afford meat more often than that. After supper Fawzia and her mother work in their home, while Ahmed goes to the coffeehouse. There he discusses village news with the other fellahin.

☆ ☆ ☆ ☆ ☆ ☆ ☆ ☆ ☆

Except for market day, an occasional wedding, or a celebration for the birth of a baby, Fawzia and her family rarely take a day off from work. Even if they

From the roof of his mosque in the Nile valley, a muezzin calls the people to prayer.

"Prayer is better than sleep...."

could afford to, they would have little reason. One day in the village is like another; nothing seems to change and few strangers ever appear. No wonder the villagers eagerly look forward to the few holidays when they can do something different.

The two biggest holidays of the Moslem year are known as the "Big Feast," and the "Little Feast." The Big Feast comes at the beginning of the ninth month of the Moslem calendar, and the Little Feast comes at the end of it. Moslems call this month *Ramadan.** It is holy to them because it was the month in which Allah began to reveal to Mohammed the words later collected in the Koran. For the entire month of Ramadan, Moslems fast during daylight hours.

Night is turned almost into day during Ramadan. From about 1 A.M. until an hour before dawn, the streets echo with the cries of a man who walks around town waking people and reminding them to eat while they can. The moment the first streak of light appears in the night sky, the fast will begin. The family cannot eat or drink again until sunset, when the fast is over for another night.

Aside from such holidays, Fawzia's days hardly change. But that does not bother her much. She is content to live out her life in her small, sunny village on the banks of the Nile. It is the only life she knows.

☆ ☆ ☆ ☆ ☆ ☆ ☆ ☆ ☆

In thousands of villages throughout the Arab world poor people live out their lives in much the same manner as Fawzia and her family. Of course, some of the villages look different. In North Africa, for example, olive groves and grape vineyards often cover the hillsides. Many North Africans depend on the vineyards for their living as much as Egyptians depend on growing grains and vegetables.

For the most part, though, the life of the Arab farmer is much the same in most areas of the Middle East. One village is much like another: the same cluster of small houses, a winding dirt street, and tiny shops. The men gather in the coffeehouse; the women meet at the well or the river's edge. In some countries — Lebanon, for example, or Kuwait — the children probably have a school to go to; in others they may not. Whether the farmers own or rent their land, their plots are always small — barely big enough for scratching out a living.

All Arab governments are training more teachers and building more schools. Many of them also have land reform programs. This means the farmers are given land of their own and taught modern farming methods. Irrigation projects — such as the construction of dams in Egypt to store the flood waters of the Nile — also help. But more time and more money are needed before these programs can have widespread results. Progress is very slow.

Fawzia will probably never leave her village. Neither will Hashem, her elder brother. His life may be somewhat easier than his father's. But he will always be a farmer who works hard to support his family.

If Hamid, the middle brother, could go on to a free public secondary school, new opportunities would then be open to him. But Hamid will probably not get past the village school, for there is no secondary school anywhere near his village. Ahmed always needs more help in the fields, and he will probably want Hamid to stay near home.

Fouad's future is a question mark. It depends on how much progress his country makes in the next several years. If Fouad and other young people like him can have the opportunity for an easier life, the Arab world may have met one of its greatest challenges.

Double-check

Review

1. Why do many Egyptian farm villages have high walls around the settlements?

2. Since ancient times, of what materials have the people of Egypt built their homes?

3. What is the duty of a muezzin?

4. What is Aswan, and why is this town important?

5. Why is the month of Ramadan holy to Moslems?

Discussion

1. Despite all its benefits, the Aswan Dam prevents silt from the upper Nile River from flowing south to enrich the farmlands of the lower Nile. Knowing its benefits and drawbacks, do you think the dam should have been built? Can you think of examples in the United States where such technological "improvements" caused environmental problems? Do you think these "improvements" should have been made? Who should make the final decisions in such situations? Explain your answers.

2. In 1952 the Egyptian government attempted to redistribute farmland from richer to poorer farmers. But today most Egyptian farmers are still poor and have small plots. Why do you suppose the government's attempt at land reform did not work? What aspects of Egyptian culture might influence farming methods?

3. Which person has a life more similar to your own — Fawzia of the Nile valley, or Hassan the Bedouin? Which one's life is most likely to change in the future? Is either person's life similar to the image you had of an Arab's life before you read these chapters? Explain your answers.

Activities

1. Some students might wish to draw a map of Egypt showing the Aswan Dam, Cairo, Alexandria, the Nile River, the Nile Delta, the Pyramids of Giza, Port Said, the Suez Canal, and Lake Nasser.

2. Several students could cooperate to assemble a scrapbook comparing farm products and tools of the Middle East and of the United States.

3. One student could play the part of Fawzia and pretend she is visiting the class. Others could interview "Fawzia" on how she feels about religion, education, the role of women, her role in her family, and her future.

Skills

WHEAT PRODUCTION IN EGYPT
1968-1982

Millions of Tons

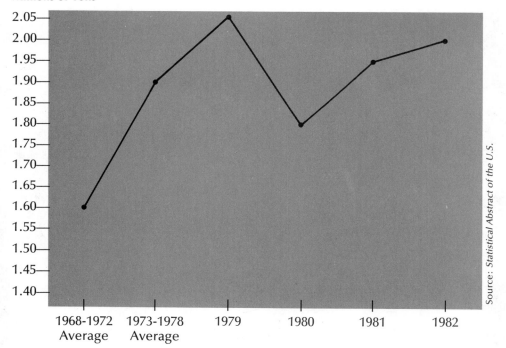

Source: *Statistical Abstract of the U.S.*

Use the line graph above and information in Chapter 4 to answer the following questions.

1. What do the numbers on the left of the graph represent?

2. What is the source of information of this graph?

3. How many tons of wheat were produced in 1980?

4. In what year was Egyptian wheat production the highest?

5. Between what two years or periods was there a decline in Egyptian wheat production? What kind of weather phenomena could account for such a decline?

2
CITY LIFE

Chapter 5

Medinas and
the Modern World

MIDDLE EASTERNERS are not city people by tradition. Until very recently, only one in three Middle Easterners lived in and around cities. In some places—Saudi Arabia or Iran, for example—that proportion was even lower. But today the Middle East is becoming more industrialized. New factories in the cities are drawing workers from the countryside. This influx is revitalizing the cities of the Middle East.

Whatever their size, the cities have always played an important role in the region. It is in the cities that Middle Eastern government, for the most part, is run. Cities are centers for artisans and, today, industrialists. They provide farmers with the large markets they need for selling their produce. In the cities, Middle Eastern music, art, architecture, and literature thrive. The region badly needs the skilled graduates turned out every year from city universities. And it is in the cities that Middle Easterners have raised to a fine art one of their favorite occupations—trade.

Many of the cities of the Middle East have histories which date back more than a thousand years. Some of them, such as Damascus,* the capital of Syria, grew up at important points on the great trade routes. Others, such as Baghdad* in Iraq and Cairo in Egypt, grew up on the banks of great rivers. Wherever they sprouted, most of these cities were built with at least two main considerations in mind.

The first was religion. Reverence for Islam led to locating the mosque at the heart of the settlement. The second need was protection — especially from Bedouin tribesmen who had the unhappy habit of raiding the settlements from time to time in search of food. To protect against these raids, cities were often built on bluffs or other hard-to-reach places and were almost always enclosed by high walls.

Inside these walls most streets were little more than crooked alleys which twisted through the heart of the city like the paths in a labyrinth. Along these streets city-dwellers built homes designed for privacy. Most stood two or three stories high, and had no windows at the street level. Higher up, windows were closely shuttered or had carved wooden screens so that people inside could look out but no one outside could look in. Most homes had inside courtyards, many of which were planted with beautiful flowers and cooled by splashing fountains.

The grander these homes became, the greater were some cities' reputations for magnificence. Wealthy landowners often moved there, living off the rents or much of the harvest of the peasants who worked the land. In Egypt rulers known as sultans built palaces and gardens in the cities. Craftsmen and small shop-

In an Algerian market, each merchant tends to be his own boss. What might be some advantages to this system? some drawbacks?

keepers sold their handmade wares — precious jewelry, rich rugs and fabrics, pottery, and other objects — in the great city marketplaces, or *bazaars*.

The streets were as noisy as they were crowded. Loaded carts creaked, camels whined, and donkeys brayed. Horses, which only the rich could afford, added to the congestion. Street merchants called out, selling fruit drinks and food on every corner. Porters offered to carry people's bundles. Beggars continually asked for money, for the Koran commands Moslems to be charitable.

A Moslem wedding party, accompanied by musicians — or a funeral procession, with loudly weeping mourners — might pass by at any moment. Buyers and sellers bargained all day in the bazaars. And five times a day, louder than all the other sounds, came the call to prayer from the minarets of all the mosques in the city.

Today new sights and new sounds have been added to the old in the cities of the Middle East. The old quarters still exist, but only as part of newer, more modern cities. Usually the old quarter is known as the *medina,** the Arabic word for "city." Within the medinas, narrow streets still snake their way past windowless homes. Ancient bazaars still serve as an outlet for merchants selling their wares.

But new cities have grown up around the old. These new cities provide sights and sounds all their own. The whining of camels and the braying of donkeys can still be heard along some city thoroughfares. But now they are frequently drowned out by the rumble of jackhammers and the tootling horns of taxicabs.

Outside the medinas, wide avenues have replaced narrow, winding streets. Autos, buses, and bicycles have slowly eased donkey carts off the streets. Apart-

✍§ To outsiders the slums are eyesores; to slum-dwellers they are graveyards of broken dreams.

ment buildings have taken the place of old, single-family homes. Hotels and office buildings have shot skyward in a Western-style salute to concrete and steel.

Around the outer rim of the downtown areas stretch the suburbs where many of those who work in the city live. Here, too, are slums — clusters of tumble-down shacks built from scraps of lumber, old tin cans, and similar materials. To outsiders the slums are eyesores; to slum-dwellers they are all-too-often graveyards of broken dreams.

Many slum-dwellers once lived as peasants in overcrowded villages. Blocked by lack of opportunity, they left their homes and came to the cities to be "in on things" — especially higher paying jobs in industry. Since they lacked industrial skills, however, many of them had to settle for low-paying jobs as household servants or day laborers. Over the years they have eked out an existence without much money and without the means of making more. By now many of them have found that city life is no better than life in the villages — that, in some ways, it is worse.

Their poverty stems partly from a problem which has plagued most of the Middle East for generations: that, except for Israel, the region lacks the industries to provide jobs for all those who want them.

One possible solution is to create more industries, and for decades these countries have been trying to do just that. But to build industry takes money and there are very few Middle Easterners who have enough of it to take chances on new industries. Those who do have money sometimes prefer to invest it elsewhere — in land, for example.

Countries without much oil income, such as Egypt, have to build the slow way. Countries with the vast new oil wealth — Iran, Saudi Arabia, and Kuwait, for example — have spent huge sums building new schools and industries.

Working hand in hand, the growth of industry and the spread of schools have brought about another change in Middle Eastern life. No longer are the cities the home of only two groups: the few very rich and the many very poor. In recent years these cities have also become the home of a growing number of doctors, lawyers, teachers, engineers, business people — all members of a rising middle class.

So, for all their many drawbacks, the cities still offer opportunities which are available nowhere else in the Arab world. As they continue to spread outward and upward, they produce the people and the goods which can help to make the region prosper.

NORTH AFRICA

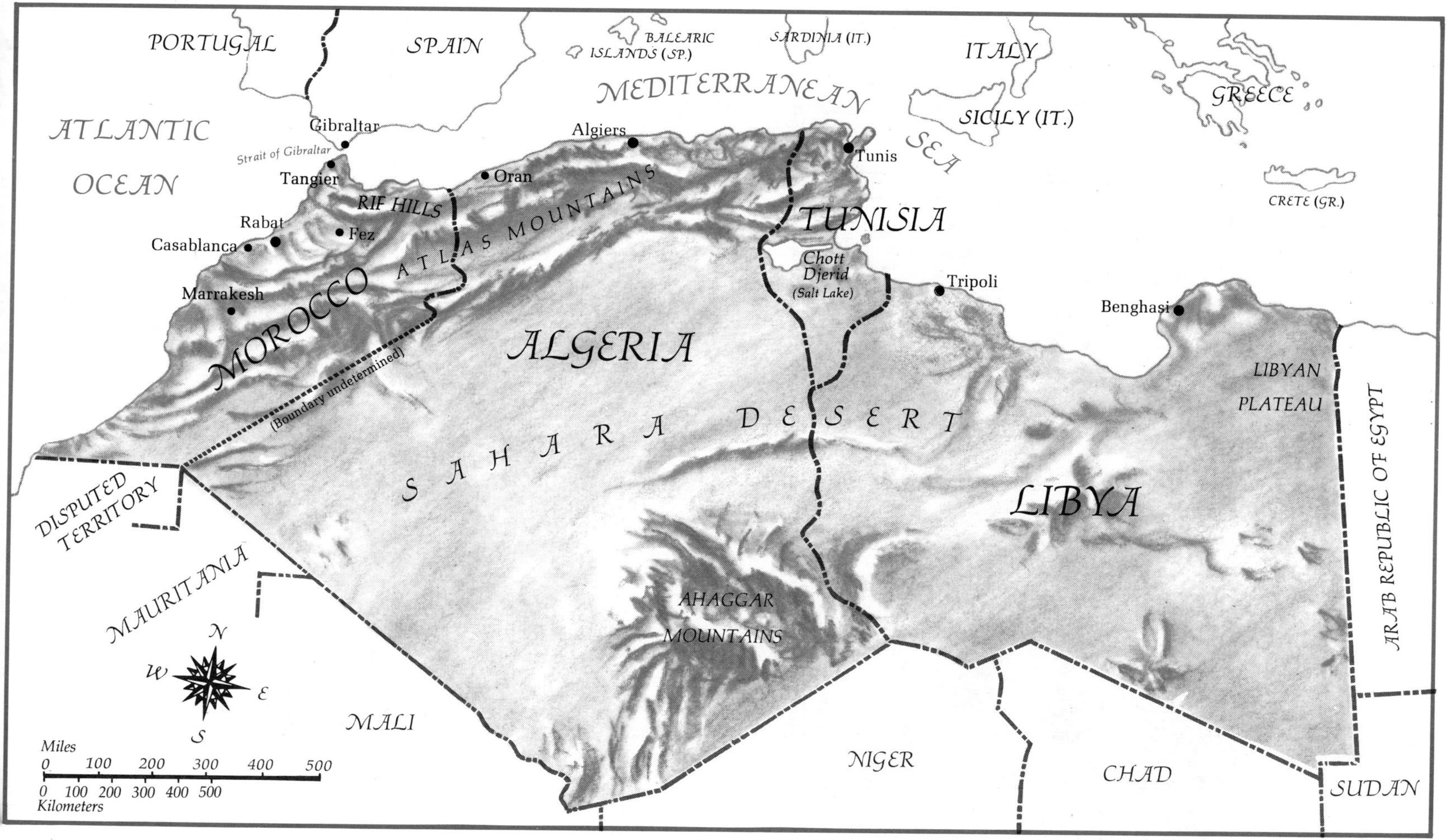

PORTUGAL

SPAIN

ATLANTIC OCEAN

GREECE

CRETE (GR.)

ITALY

SICILY (IT.)

SARDINIA (IT.)

BALEARIC ISLANDS (SP.)

MEDITERRANEAN SEA

ARAB REPUBLIC OF EGYPT

SUDAN

LIBYAN PLATEAU

Benghasi

LIBYA

CHAD

Tripoli

TUNISIA

Tunis

Chott Djerid (Salt Lake)

S A H A R A   D E S E R T

NIGER

Algiers

ALGERIA

Oran

ATLAS MOUNTAINS

AHAGGAR MOUNTAINS

Gibraltar

Strait of Gibraltar

Tangier

RIF HILLS

Fez

Rabat

MOROCCO

Casablanca

Marrakesh

(boundary undetermined)

MALI

DISPUTED TERRITORY

MAURITANIE

N
W   E
S

Miles
0   100   200   300   400   500
0   100   200   300   400   500
Kilometers

For a knowledge of the stars, European scientists relied heavily on Arab astronomers, shown in this old European woodcut.

THE ARABS COME FORTH

LONG BEFORE the Arab-Israeli hostilities of the present day, another war in the Middle East made history. This war took place more than 1,300 years ago, but it, too, brought great changes to the area. This time the conquerors were Arabs.

The outside world then knew little about the Arabs. They came from a land few had seen, a place so blisteringly hot and forbiddingly dry that the great conquerors of the past — Babylonians,* Persians, Greeks, and Romans — had shunned it. Suddenly, about the year 633 A.D., the Arabs burst upon the world scene, leaving their mark throughout the Middle East and beyond.

Their armies were made up of Bedouin tribesmen who had roamed the deserts of Arabia in search of grass and water for their camels, horses, and goats. For centuries the Bedouins had fought among themselves. And for centuries they had raided tribes living on the borders of Arabia and taken away their cattle.

It was Mohammed, with his new religion, who united the Arab tribes and organized them into armies. Between 622 and 632 A.D., thousands of Bedouins converted to the new faith. In adopting it, they also adopted one of its basic teachings — that Moslem must never fight Moslem. The more widely Islam took hold in Arabia, the farther afield Bedouin warriors had to go to find non-Moslem people to plunder.

In 633 they invaded Syria, an area which then included the present-day nations of Syria, Jordan, Lebanon, and Israel. The hard life of the Bedouins had toughened them and made them expert fighters; their new faith, Islam, molded them into fearless men with a mission. In Syria the Bedouins faced the troops of a great military power, the Byzantine* Empire. The Byzantines were far more numerous and far better armed than the Bedouins.

Yet the Arabs won the opening battles. Mounted on camels and horses, they charged furiously into the enemy lines again and again. Then in hand-to-hand combat they finished off their foes. Almost all of Syria, including the capital city of Damascus, fell to the Arabs.

One of the last cities to hold out was Jerusalem. To the Arabs, as to the Jews and Christians, Jerusalem was a holy city, for one of the most revered places of Islam was located there. Moslems believed that only a few years earlier Mohammed, astride a winged animal, had used a rock in Jerusalem as a steppingstone to ascend into heaven. To conquer the city and gain control of the rock now became an important Arab goal.

Slowly the Arabs tightened the knot, hemming in the city with their other conquests. In 638 Jerusalem finally fell. The man who accepted its surrender was an Arab leader named Omar,* whom Moslems called *caliph**
(meaning the "successor" to Mohammed). He entered the city and hurried to pray at the sacred rock.

Those first victories in Syria proved only a beginning for the Arabs. During the next century they conquered Egypt and all of North Africa. Then they crossed the

Strait of Gibraltar* and conquered the Iberian Peninsula, today's Spain and Portugal. Their armies even pushed into southern France before they were defeated and turned back at the Battle of Tours in 732.

Nor did Arab warriors confine themselves only to the Middle East. They swept north through the lands now called Iran and Iraq, and east as far as India and the borders of China. Where Arab fighters did not go, Arab tradesmen often did. Over the course of several centuries, these tradesmen worked their way down the Malay Peninsula of Southeast Asia and onto the islands that now make up Indonesia and the Philippines.

Into every country they went, the Arabs took their language and religion. In time they spread Islam halfway around the globe from Morocco in the west to Indonesia in the east. They also spread the Arabic language across most of the Middle East (although other languages — Turkish, Persian, and Berber, for example — continued to prevail in large areas). The Middle East now became mainly an Arab domain.

The capital of this domain was the city of Baghdad. At Baghdad, between 750 and 850 A.D., Arab culture reached its most elaborate heights. That city gained fame for its wealth and splendor, as depicted in the tales of *The Arabian Nights*.

It also gained fame for its scholarship. At a time when Europe was sunk in the Dark Ages, Arab scholars were swapping ideas of a more advanced sort. In particular, they studied Indian mathematics and Greek medicine, geometry, and science. Arab scholars made one of their most important contributions by translating into Arabic the works of the ancient Greeks. When Europeans first "discovered" the works of Greek scientists hundreds of years later, they read those works in Arabic.

In the 13th century, the grandeur of the Arab world began to fade. Other conquerors came and left their mark on the Middle East. Baghdad fell to ruins as dusty as the nearby desert. In 1492 Arab armies were finally driven from Spain. But the accomplishments of the Arab empire at its height have lived on in memory and legend.

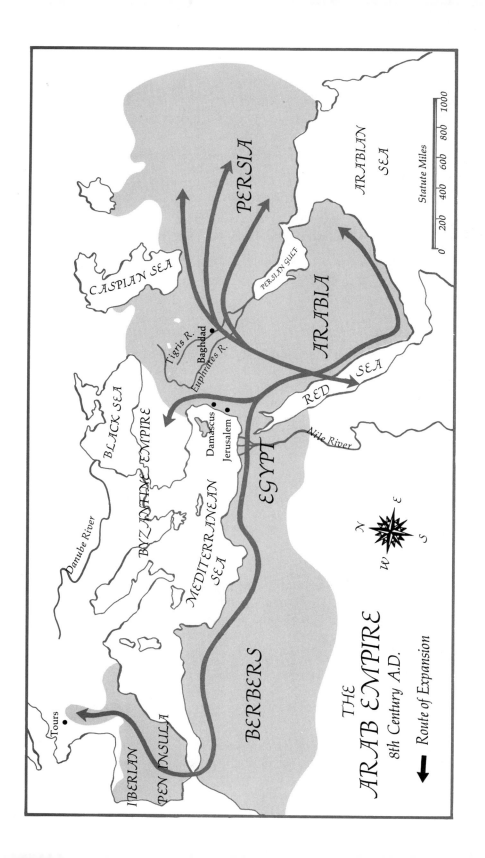

THE
ARAB EMPIRE
8th Century A.D.

→ Route of Expansion

Statute Miles
0 200 400 600 800 1000

PERSIA

ARABIAN
SEA

CASPIAN SEA

Tigris R.
Baghdad
Euphrates R.

PERSIAN GULF

ARABIA

RED SEA

BLACK SEA

BYZANTINE EMPIRE

Damascus
Jerusalem

EGYPT

Nile River

Danube River

MEDITERRANEAN
SEA

BERBERS

IBERIAN
PENINSULA

Tours

N
W   E
S

Double-check

Review

1. Up until recently, what fraction of Middle Easterners lived in or around urban areas?

2. To protect against Bedouin raids, where were Middle Eastern cities often built?

3. What does the word *medina* mean in English?

4. What happened to the Arabs at the Battle of Tours in 732 A.D.?

5. What was the capital city of the Arab domain between 750 and 850 A.D.?

Discussion

1. Poverty, unemployment, and lack of good housing remain as major problems for cities of the Middle East. What efforts can these cities make to solve the problems? What efforts have U.S. cities — including your own — made to solve these problems? Do you think these problems can be solved? If so, how? If not, why not?

2. In a relatively short time, the Arabs were able to extend their empire from Spain to Indonesia. Why do you suppose the Arabs were so effective in spreading their religion and culture?

3. How do you suppose our lives might have been different if there never had been a great age of Arab civilization at the time when Europe was "sunk in the Dark Ages"?

Activities

1. Students who like to draw might make sketches of life in various cities of the Middle East. Others could research Middle Eastern architecture and draw public and private buildings. Some students could research and report on why their own city or other U.S. cities were founded where they were.

2. Some students might work together in constructing a timeline of Arab history from the birth of Mohammed to the year 1492. They should be sure to include on this timeline important dates and events mentioned in the chapter.

3. Other students might wish to research and write a report on contributions made by Arabs during the golden age of Arab civilization. Possible subjects could include astronomy, art, architecture, medicine, geometry, science, and literature.

Skills

POPULATION DENSITY OF SEVERAL MIDDLE EASTERN COUNTRIES

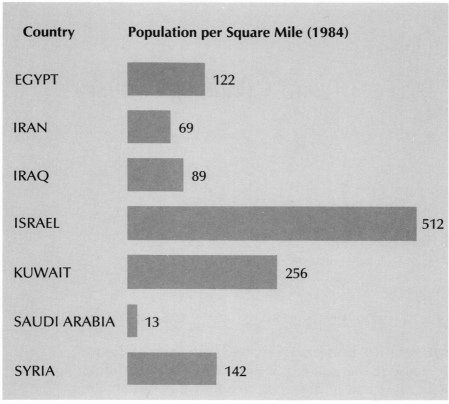

Country	Population per Square Mile (1984)
EGYPT	122
IRAN	69
IRAQ	89
ISRAEL	512
KUWAIT	256
SAUDI ARABIA	13
SYRIA	142

Source: *Statistical Abstract of the U.S.*

Use the bar graph above and information in Chapter 5 to answer the following questions.

1. What do the bars represent? For what year is the information given?

2. According to the graph, what does population density mean?

3. If 10 square miles of land in Saudi Arabia conformed to the national average, how many people would be living there?

4. Which two Middle Eastern countries shown have the densest populations?

5. Do all the countries shown which have vast new oil wealth have high population density?

Chapter 6

Cairo: Citadel of Change

MUNIR,* 14, LIVES in Cairo, the largest city of Egypt. It is also the largest city in all Africa and the Middle East, and one of the most modern capitals in the world. Three hundred miles to the south, Fawzia and her family in the Nile valley live in much the same way as their ancestors did when Cairo was new a thousand years ago. But Munir's life differs even from the way his grandparents lived.

Munir and his sister, Safiya,* 12, live with their parents in a five-room apartment. Their apartment house sits on an island in the middle of the Nile, just where the river passes through the center of Cairo. The island is a little more than two miles long, less than a half mile wide, and has many modern apartment buildings.

*Moslem students and teachers at one of the
world's oldest universities, al-Azhar in Cairo.*

The apartment Munir lives in is like one in a Western country. Instead of floor cushions there are tables and chairs, and instead of sleeping mats, there are beds. The kitchen has running water, and an electric range and a refrigerator. In the living room is a television set. Munir and Safiya have their own radios.

In the morning, the calls of the muezzins from Cairo's many mosques boom over loudspeakers. The day begins later than it does in the rural areas of the Nile valley, but not as late as in a Western country. Schools and offices are already busy by seven or eight o'clock, so breakfast is early.

Munir eats breakfast in the dining room, on a chair at the table. He knows the old Arab way of eating. He has visited a village in the fertile Nile Delta, the farm area just north of Cairo, where his grandfather was a headman. There he has seen people eat with their fingers, everyone taking his food from a single dish. But Munir's family table is set as in Western countries, with knives, forks, and spoons.

In one way, though, Munir's breakfast is likely to be similar to Fawzia's — it very often includes brown beans. The beans are cooked in oil and well seasoned. But where Fawzia's family will sell any eggs its chickens lay, Munir's family often has eggs for breakfast.

Munir's father works for the Egyptian government. He is a farm expert and member of the department which helps fellahin to increase their crop production. Munir is in his third and last year in a preparatory school, which is like the ninth grade of a junior high school in the United States. He studies history, science, mathematics, the Koran, and English as well as Arabic. Next year he will begin three years of high school. Then he plans to enter Cairo University.

Munir thinks the Arabic he is studying is just as

difficult as a foreign language. This is because it is the written "classical" Arabic of the Koran. It differs from the ordinary spoken Arabic that Munir and his family speak. For Munir, learning classical Arabic is somewhat like an American student learning to speak the English that was spoken in England hundreds of years ago.

Safiya is still in elementary school. Her school is co-ed, but next year, when she begins the preparatory course, she will go to a girls' school. In all Egyptian preparatory and high schools, girls and boys study separately.

Munir and Safiya travel to school by bus. Their section of Cairo is the newest part of the city. Most of the people there wear Western-style clothes, as do Munir and his family. Safiya is dressed in her school uniform — blouse, skirt, and jacket. Munir wears a dark suit.

Now and then Munir sees someone in the crowd wearing the traditional robes of the Egyptian villagers. A man selling cold Pepsi-Cola at an umbrella-covered street stand is dressed this way. But his costume looks old-fashioned next to the new banks, department stores, and office buildings in this part of town.

Far across the city to the east is the Citadel, or fortress, built 800 years ago. There things look quite different. Students can be seen on their way to one of the oldest educational institutions in the world, al-Azhar* University. Al-Azhar was founded a thousand years ago by the Arab conquerors in Egypt. Although many new buildings have been added, the oldest one, the mosque of al-Azhar, is still the center of the university. At al-Azhar many classes are held in the old mosque itself. There the students sit on rugs on the ground, grouped around their teacher.

Schools, offices, and shops in large Egyptian cities such as Cairo close early in the afternoon. Work usually stops by two o'clock, and people start home for a leisurely lunch and a long rest. The hottest hours of the day are in the early afternoon, and everyone wants to be indoors and out of the sun. Businessmen usually start back to work about four o'clock and stay at their desks or tend their shops until about eight in the evening.

In the villages girls and boys, unless they belong to the same family, are usually kept apart before marriage. This isn't usually true any more in Cairo or other large Egyptian cities. Some of the school clubs to which Munir and Safiya belong include both boys and girls. But neither Munir nor Safiya goes out on dates alone.

Safiya knows that most Egyptian parents pick out husbands for their daughters. She vows that, when the time comes, she is going to choose her husband for herself. But first she wants to go to Cairo University.

The family has dinner, the main meal of the day, together at home. Moslems do not eat pork, but they eat a great deal of lamb and chicken. Pigeon and fish are popular, too. Since the villagers keep their cows as work animals, there is not much beef. Most often, Munir and his family have lamb for dinner. Munir's mother serves this as *kebab** — bite-size pieces flavored with garlic and cooked on skewers. With it there are vegetables and a salad, and for dessert, fruit — perhaps watermelon or cantaloupe — or pastry. Arab pastry is sweet and rich, made with sugar, butter, almonds or pine nuts, and much honey. With dinner the family drinks strong tea or coffee.

Then comes the best time for enjoying oneself in Cairo — the long evening. People tend to stay up late in Egyptian cities. They have had a long rest in the afternoon, and they like to take advantage of the cool nights.

Neither Safiya nor her mother goes out alone in the evenings, but the family may go out together. Sometimes they go to a play or a concert, and sometimes just to the movies. These family outings often take place on Thursday nights, which are like Saturday nights in the U.S. Friday is the Moslem day of rest, just as Saturday is the Jewish day of rest and Sunday the Christian day of rest.

On some Thursday nights the family joins the strollers along the tree-lined streets. People buy fruit drinks and roasted corn-on-the-cob from street vendors. Little boats with tall sails glide up and down the Nile, taking people on tours of the river.

Munir thinks his city is beautiful at night, but most beautiful during the nights of Ramadan. All day long many people have fasted, and at sundown they are ready to enjoy themselves. Restaurants and cafes bustle with activity until dawn. Shops do not close, and theaters have late shows. Music and merrymaking are everywhere.

In the midst of the gaiety, people do not forget to pray. Crowds flock to the mosques, kept open all night during this month. The minarets are lighted and their reflection sparkles on the Nile. At this time of year two Cairos are on view — the new and modern one where Munir lives, and the old and fabled one where the sultans ruled, surrounded by "all the delights of this life."

Double-check

Review

1. By what time in the morning are schools and offices in Cairo busy?

2. When, and by whom, was al-Azhar University founded?

3. What are the meats that Munir and his family eat most often?

4. Why do people tend to stay up late in Egyptian cities?

5. What day is the Moslem day of rest?

Discussion

1. Compare life in the three different places you have studied so far: Hassan's "house of hair" tent, Fawzia's mud brick house, and Munir's city apartment. How do these dwellings compare with the one in which you live? In which of them would you most like to live? Least like to live? Why?

2. In what ways is Munir's life similar to Fawzia's? In what ways are their lives different? Do you think that growing up in the countryside or in a city makes any difference in the type of career that Egyptian — or American — young people choose? Should it make a difference?

3. In Cairo, people arise early and stay up late, but they rest in the afternoon. For what reasons do they schedule their days this way? Why do you schedule your day the way you do? How is it different from a typical Egyptian's day? Which do you prefer? Why?

Activities

1. Some students could pretend they are tourists in Cairo and write a travel diary about the differences they notice between life in Cairo and life in their own city or town. Some of the "tourists" could write about visiting Cairo during the month of Ramadan.

2. A committee of students might watch television and read newspapers and magazines for reports of current events in Cairo. Articles, photos, and political cartoons could be displayed on a bulletin board under appropriate headings.

3. Several students could research why and when Cairo was founded, how the city is laid out, what historic events have happened there, and what famous buildings and gardens Cairo has. Then they could make an oral report to the class.

Skills

TYPES OF COMMUNICATIONS IN THE MIDDLE EAST

Country	Telephones in use	Daily Newspaper Circulation	Radios in Use	TV Sets in Use
EGYPT	534	2,475	6,000	1,400
IRAN	1,227	(NA)	2,050	2,085
ISRAEL	1,130	801	802	581
MOROCCO	231	230	3,000	749
SAUDI ARABIA	443	143	2,500	2,100
TURKEY	1,902	3,880	4,284	3,348
(all numbers in thousands)				

Source: *Statistical Abstract of the U.S.*

Use the table above and information in Chapter 6 to answer the following questions.

1. What do the numbers in the table stand for?

2. How many television sets were in use in Morocco in 1980?

3. In what category is it impossible to tell which country ranks first or last?

4. Is the largest city in the Middle East located in a country that has the greatest number of radios?

Chapter 7

Fez: The Tread of the Past

IN SOME WAYS Munir has quite a bit in common with
another Arab teenager, Khaled.* Both are Moslems,
and both are the same age, 14. Like Munir, Khaled
lives in an Arab country, Morocco. Like Munir,
Khaled lives in a city, Fez. But the similarities stop
there, for Khaled's life is very different from Munir's.

Parts of Fez are as modern as the part of Cairo in
which Munir lives. For about 50 years, until 1956,
the French ruled Morocco. In Fez they built wide,
tree-lined avenues and Western-style houses, hotels,
and office buildings. But the part of Fez in which
Khaled lives is the oldest section, the medina, and it is
separated from the newer city by an ancient wall.

The old town is almost 1,200 years old. About the
year 800 the first Arab ruler of Morocco, a great-
grandson of Mohammed, founded Fez. The narrow
streets are either dirt or paved with cobblestones.
Because the old town is built on a hillside most of the
streets slope steeply. Some have steps built into them.
Most homes have no windows at all facing on the
street.

84

Just outside the medina walls, buses speed by on the modern streets of the newer city. Inside there is no room even for automobiles. Instead, donkeys and bicycles jam the lanes.

Khaled's family has lived in the medina for generations. The men in the family have always earned their living as leather toolers, making delicate designs by hand on leather goods such as bookcovers, briefcases, and belts. Many of the designs are made in 18-carat gold. Fez is well known for fine leather and for the kind of leather work which Khaled's family does.

Khaled's father, Haroun,* inherited his leather tools from his father, who taught Haroun his craft. Khaled's older brother, Syed,* who is 25, learned from Haroun, and now Khaled is learning, too. In Khaled's family, fathers have always taught their sons the family trade.

Haroun's shop is in the bazaar area of the old town. Shops which sell similar kinds of goods are grouped together on the the same street in the bazaar. Haroun's shop is on the Street of the Leather Workers. There is also the Street of the Leather Makers, where Haroun buys the leather he uses in his work.

On the Street of the Coppersmiths, gleaming bowls, pitchers, and cups are hammered into shape by hand. Along the Street of the Dyers, bright skeins of red and yellow wool hang overhead, newly dyed and drying, later to be woven into rugs. On the Street of the Potters, the shops contain shelf after shelf of beautiful jars and vases in many shapes and colors — deep aquamarine, or designs of blue, yellow, red, and white. Along other streets merchants sell spices, perfumes, objects of brass, fabrics, gold and silver jewelry, and embroidery. They also sell prayer rugs, small carpets which many Moslems kneel on when they pray.

**⋖§ Along the Street of the Dyers,
bright skeins of wool hang overhead,
later to be woven into rugs.**

Like the other shops, Haroun's is small and has an open front. It holds his work bench and a few shelves to display his goods, with little space for anything else. Some shops are even smaller — where some of the cloth-weavers sit working, the ceilings are so low that it is impossible to stand up.

Nearby is the home of Khaled's family. The house is made of stone, covered with whitewashed cement. It is one story high and has five large rooms. There is a courtyard in the center on which all the rooms open. Khaled, his parents, and his two sisters and younger brother live in two of the rooms, and his older brother Syed and Syed's wife and two young children live in the other two. The fifth room is the kitchen, which both families share.

From the outside most houses in the medina look alike. But inside they may be quite different. The homes of the rich have beautiful fountains and large gardens in their courtyards. The floors and walls of their many rooms are covered with beautiful painted tiles, and tables and chests are hand-carved. But most poor families live in houses of one or two rooms with little furniture or decoration.

Khaled and his family eat in traditional Arab style, sitting on the floor around a low, round table. With every meal they drink the most popular beverage in Morocco, mint tea. Moroccans take great care in making and serving tea, just as the Bedouins do with their coffee. Fresh mint leaves and tea leaves are placed in a silver or copper teapot, and boiling water

Dyed wool dries along Street of Dyers in Marrakesh, Morocco.

and a great deal of sugar are added. The tea is served in tiny glasses.

Khaled and his brother both attend public elementary school. Since Morocco became independent of France in 1956, all children are required by law to go to elementary school. Khaled is in his last year. His sisters went to school, too, although the oldest one went for only a few years. When she was younger, not enough schools had yet been built in Morocco, and many children could not attend at all. Many children still don't. Except in cities such as Fez, there still aren't enough schools.

Khaled studies most of the same subjects as Munir does, but he studies in two languages, French and Arabic. He is taught mathematics and science in French, and history and geography in Arabic. Most Moroccans speak French as well as Arabic, having learned it during the time of French rule.

Sometimes Khaled hears a third language. This is Berber, the language of the people who lived in Morocco and elsewhere in North Africa before the Arabs came. Many modern Moroccans are descendants of both Berbers and Arabs.

Other Moroccans who live in the countryside and the mountain villages have very little Arab blood. This is especially true of the people of the Rif hills of northern Morocco and of the Atlas Mountains which cut through the central and southern parts of the country. At the time of the Arab invasions, these people kept to themselves and did not mix with the Arabs. They still speak the old Berber language and follow many of the old Berber customs. Berbers, for example, never marry their first cousins, as the Arabs sometimes do. Even though the Berbers became Moslems, Berber women, when among their fellow Berbers, never wear veils.

*In a region lacking fertile land for farming,
Middle Easterners long ago became experts
in another occupation — trade. This alert Arab
merchant makes his living by selling grain.*

In his free time Khaled likes to go to the movies,
where many of the films are French or Egyptian. He
and his friends like to play soccer. Sometimes he lis-
tens to popular music from the Western countries,
especially the United States and France.

Khaled's sisters spend most of their time at home
with their mother. They like the movies as much as
Khaled does, but they never go to such public places
unless their father or one of their brothers takes them.
Outdoors they usually wear veils.

Haroun will probably choose husbands for his daughters soon, although they often joke about picking out their own. Haroun says "maybe," but they will have to be boys well known to the family — relatives or the sons of close friends. Haroun believes the old way of doing things is still the best way for his daughters.

Sometimes Khaled thinks about planning a life different from the old way. Once he wanted to learn all about his father's work and to join Haroun and Syed in the shop. Now he knows that there are many other things he might do for a living.

Haroun is proud of his two sons in school. When he was young, the only book to be studied was the Koran. In studying the Koran, students learned to read and write. Thus they were better off than most children who only learned to memorize verses from the Koran. Now Haroun doesn't seem to mind when Khaled talks about new ways of doing things. He does not mind when Khaled says he does not want to become a leather worker like Haroun.

Haroun knows that few of the old handcrafts are left. Much of what is sold in the bazaar now is machine-made. There are very few customers for hand-tooled leather and handmade rugs and pottery — most of the customers are tourists. Many Moroccans buy the new factory-made goods, which cost much less. In 20 years — or perhaps in only 10 or five — there may not be much of a living to be made from leather work.

Haroun would like to see Khaled leave the medina and go out into the newer city to live another kind of life. Khaled's education is giving him the chance to do this.

Double-check

Review

1. About when and by whom was the city of Fez founded?

2. What is the most popular beverage in Morocco?

3. Berber is the language of what people?

4. What mountain range cuts through central and southern Morocco?

5. When Haroun was young, what book did he study?

Discussion

1. Morocco was a French colony for many decades. How do you suppose that being a French colony has influenced the kind of country Morocco is today? Do you think that being a French colony has made Morocco different from Egypt or Saudi Arabia, and similar to Algeria (which was also a French colony)? How has the United States been influenced by being a former English colony? Explain your answers.

2. How can getting an education help Khaled live a life different from that of his father? What might Khaled do for a living if he decides to move to the newer city? Do you think that Khaled should become a leather worker like his father? If you were Khaled, would you want to move to the newer city? Explain your answers.

3. In the United States, there has been increased interest in handcrafts in recent decades. Why do you suppose this is so? Do you think handcrafts in Morocco will again become more popular and profitable? Why, or why not?

Activities

1. Some students might research and write reports on aspects of the history or government of Morocco.

2. Other students might create a bulletin board display titled "Life in Modern Morocco." Students could display pictures of the people, crafts, costumes, buildings, terrain, foods, and other aspects of life in Morocco today.

3. Some students might learn about one of the crafts mentioned in the chapter and give reports or demonstrations on the craft. Students could compare artistic styles in the Middle East and the United States in these crafts.

Skills

USING AN INDEX

Use the above listings from the index to this book and information in Chapter 7 to answer the following questions.

1. In what order are topics listed in an index?
  (a) by importance   (b) by page number   (c) alphabetically

2. On what page would you find an illustration of a muezzin?
  (a) 57   (b) 78   (c) 33

3. On how many pages in this text are mosques discussed?
  (a) 29   (b) two   (c) three

4. On what page is the first mention of Morocco?
  (a) 18   (b) 14   (c) 84

5. Which of the following subtopics shown on this index page describes the subject matter of Chapter 7?
  (a) life in Fez   (b) Moses   (c) mosques

Chapter 8

Teheran: Nightingales and Revolution

CONTRASTS ABOUND THROUGHOUT the Middle East, but in Teheran the capital of Iran, they are especially sharp. Teheran is a dizzying mixture of the old and the new. It is a metropolis of glass-walled skyscrapers, blinking neon lights, and traffic-clogged streets. Iranian motorists tend to drive with a carefree attitude, and are noted more for their skill in steering around obstacles than for their care or courtesy.

Yet along these same streets walk Iranian women draped in huge scarf-like coverings. These long dark veils, called *chadors*, are traditional Islamic garments, designed to conceal a woman's face and body when she is outside her home. Since the Iranian Revolution of 1979, the government has told women to wear the chador, and most do. Islamic law is the law of the land in this oil-rich nation.

Yasmine,* who lives in Teheran, is a Moslem like 98 percent of her compatriots, but she is not an Arab. Iran is not an Arab country. Most Iranians trace their heritage back to the Aryans, a people who moved into the region 4,000 years ago. The name Iran means "land of the Aryans." The Greeks called the land Persia, and this name stuck in the West. But Iranians have always called their homeland Iran. Arab Moslems conquered the land in the seventh century, and since then Islam has been the religion of the Iranian people.

Yasmine lives in an elegant apartment on the north side of Teheran. The apartment's floors are covered with deeply colored persian rugs woven to ancient patterns.

Once a week, Yasmine and her family visit her grandparents in an old, walled house in another part of town. Yasmine loves the tiny gardens at the house and the songs of the nightingales her grandmother keeps. Once a familiar tradition in Iranian life, nightingales are disappearing. Today, few people seem to have time to care for such fragile birds.

In recent years, much has changed in the lives of Iranians. Yasmine and her family are unusual because they are wealthy, but they too have experienced much that is new. Yasmine's grandparents were once among the richest and most powerful people in Iran and they owned large tracts of land in the northern part of the country. Like many members of Iran's nobility, they seldom visited their lands. Their agents collected the large rents from the peasants who farmed the land. It was customary to divide harvests under a "five-fifths" system. The crop was divided into five shares—one each for the persons supplying the land, water, seed, equipment, and labor. Since the landlord usually supplied the first four, he got four fifths of the harvest. The farmer, who supplied only the labor, ended up with just one fifth. The result of this system was that the largest portion of Iran's population was desperately poor and was tied to the land almost like serfs.

During the 1960's and 70's Iran's leader, Shah Mo-

*A world apart from the glitter of the cities,
life in Iran's villages moves to a slower beat.
Above, a group of farmers gather by the mud-
baked walls of their village to exchange news.*

hammed Riza Pahlevi tried to reform this pattern of land-holding. But the pace was very slow. Few land-owners willingly gave up such easy income, even though the Iranian government offered to buy out the wealthy landowners. But Yasmine's grandparents accepted the offer in 1972. They put the money from the sale in real estate investments, especially in Teheran. As Iran's economy boomed, these investments became very valuable.

Iran's economic boom resulted mainly from the vast amount of money coming into the country through the sale of oil. Iran sits on top of about 10 percent of the world's known oil reserves. And before 1979, Iran was the world's second largest exporter of oil (behind Saudi Arabia). This wealth drew into Teheran investors from all over the world and led to a tremendous building boom in the city.

But despite the reforming spirit and successful economic policies of the shah's government, many Iranians were unhappy with their ruler. The shah promoted education, improved schools and hospitals, and gave women the vote, but he also ruled the country as a dictator. He allowed little open opposition to his policies. His secret police, the dreaded Savak, sought out political opponents and often killed or imprisoned them. Many of the shah's reforms benefited only the rich. He and his close associates became extremely wealthy while the majority of Iranians lived in poverty. Also, conservative Muslims believed his modernization programs were against traditional Islamic teachings.

Opposition to the shah's regime came to a head in 1979. After massive demonstrations against him the shah left the country in January. Islamic revolutionaries led by the Ayatollah Ruhollah Khomeini took over the country and declared it an Islamic republic. Thousands of Iranians with ties to the shah fled the country.

The United States was the shah's closest ally, and many Iranians were angry when President Jimmy Carter allowed the shah to enter the United States for medical treatment. In November of 1979, a large group of Iranians stormed the U.S. embassy in Teheran and seized Americans as hostages. They demanded the shah be returned to Iran for "trial and punishment." When the demand was refused, the hostages were held prisoners, despite almost worldwide condemnation of the action.

The shah voluntarily left the U.S. in December 1979 and died seven months later in Egypt. But the American hostages were not released until January 20, 1981. These events isolated Iran from most other nations of the world, even other Moslem nations.

Inside Iran since the revolution, life has remained restricted. Khomeini's party, the Islamic Republican Party, is the only party officially allowed, and his political opponents have been executed or jailed. Western newspapers, TV shows, and plays have been declared anti-Islamic and banned. Also, the economic boom has faded. Poor Iranians face the same problems they had under the shah: bad housing and high food prices.

One cause of Iran's economic problems is its fierce and ongoing war with neighboring Iraq. This war, which broke out over a border dispute in 1980, is a constant drain on Iran's material and human resources. Iraq is richer and better armed, but Khomeini has refused to give up the fight which he regards as a "holy struggle." Iran has lost over 100,000 soldiers in battle.

Despite the hardships of everyday life, most Iranians are content enough. Few predict another revolution like the one in 1979. One Iranian explained it this way: "We are happy with the combination of old and new we have now. We keep alive the traditions and ideas of the past."

Double-check

Review

1. What is the capital city of Iran?

2. What does the name *Iran* mean in English?

3. Since what event has Islam been the religion of the Iranians?

4. About what percentage of the world's oil reserves does Iran have?

5. What event in 1979 caused the shah to lose power and flee the country?

Discussion

1. When the Ayatollah Khomeini came to power in Iran, many women went back to wearing veils, and job opportunities for women lessened. Why do you think these changes were made? How might you have felt about these changes if you were a woman in Iran at the time? What, if anything, do these changes say about Iranian women's political power?

2. Do you think the "five-fifths" system of dividing harvests was fair to farmers? Why, or why not? How do you think the system arose? Why do you think the farmers accepted it for so many years? How was the "five-fifths" system similar to, and different from, the sharecropping system used in the United States?

3. How would you feel toward the new regime in Iran if you were Yasmine or her grandparents? What people in Iran supported the revolution? Do you think the revolution has benefited people in Iran? Explain your answers.

Activities

1. Some students might create a map of Iran which depicts its mountain ranges, rivers, cities, major bodies of water, and major oil fields.

2. Iran is famous for its hand-woven "Persian" carpets. Some students might bring pictures of these carpets to school. Other students could research and report to the class on how these carpets are made and designed.

3. Students might role-play a debate between the shah and the ayatollah on the subject "Modernization Is Good for Iran."

Skills

THE AYATOLLAH KHOMEINI SPEAKS

*In Islam we want to implement a policy
to purify society, and in order to achieve
this aim, we must punish those who
bring evil to our youth. Don't you do the
same? When a thief is a thief, don't you
throw him in jail? In many countries,
don't you even execute murderers?
Don't you use that system because, if
they were to remain free and alive, they
would contaminate others and spread
their stain of wickedness?*

— interview with Western journalist, 1979

*Use the passage above and information in Chapter 8 to answer the
following questions.*

1. Under what circumstances did Khomeini say these words?
   (a) in a speech   (b) in an interview   (c) on a radio show

2. What is the main topic of this passage?
   (a) punishment of criminals   (b) Iranian youth   (c) jails

3. When Khomeini uses "you," whom does he mean?
   (a) the journalist   (b) the Western world   (c) criminals

4. According to the passage, how should criminals be treated?
   (a) turned free   (b) rehabilitated   (c) punished

5. Who is the Ayatollah Khomeini?

THE LAND

As landscapes go, the Middle East is marked by contrasts. There are forests and mountains. Nature has also given the region spectacular, unbroken horizons, widest of all in the great Sahara (left) and along the Mediterranean Sea (below).

WATER: From the scrubby highlands of Turkey (far right) to the desert plains of Egypt (lower right), water is the lifeblood of the Middle East. For water, farmers rely on rivers such as the Jordan (below). But even some rivers go dry (right), and farmers must irrigate.

STRUCTURES: Many Middle Eastern structures
seem to spring from their natural surroundings
— and some actually do. Top left, Roman ruins
in Jordan. Bottom left, 1,200-year-old city of
Shibbam in Saudi Arabian desert. Above, Turkish
cave-dweller's home hewn from volcanic debris.

HOMES: Many Arabs dwell in cities such as
Cairo (below). A handful of the wealthiest live in
ornate palaces (above). But the vast majority
of Middle Easterners live in dusty villages
such as the one in Morocco pictured at left.

THE PEOPLE

Like people everywhere, Middle Easterners look forward to the small joys that make a life of hard work more bearable. Those joys may include a leisurely spin on the family hay wagon (left) or the chance to watch in wonder while the local magician runs through his list of tricks (below).

FACES: Lost in thought, locked in alarm, or lined with curiosity, Middle Eastern faces are a mosaic of attitudes and features. Left, Nile Valley peasants. Above, a Bedouin woman in Jordan. Right, cafe patrons in the city of Fez, Morocco.

AT EASE: Middle Easterners get special pleasure from the things they do with family or friends — whether it be a coffee break among elderly Turks (left), a baby-ogling lunch break in Israel (bottom left), or a family dinner in Tunisia (below). But even super-social people sometimes stray off into their own worlds like the Egyptian at right.

URBAN TEENS: Young people in Tel Aviv (top left) and Cairo (bottom left) socialize. Above, Tehran girls chant slogans for the fundamentalist revolution, which will bring compulsory veiling. Below, Egyptian university students smile for an American visitor.

THE ECONOMY

"We are still struggling to bring our countries into the 20th century," says one Arab official. Part of the answer is trade, which now links past and present in a variety of ways. The past lingers in ancient bazaars such as the one in Tunis (left). The present pops up amid oil pipelines which cover Kuwait City docks (below).

FOOD: *Where much of the land is lifeless, people prize whatever food and livestock they have. Moroccan shepherds inspect goats (above). Iraqi fisherman prepares to cast a net into the historic Tigris River (top right). Egyptian fellahin women sort out corn (bottom right).*

CLOTHING: Textiles are a major thread
in the expanding loom of Middle Eastern
industry. An Iranian woman checks spindles
for making burlap (above). An Israeli
designer creates textile patterns (top right).
Egyptians sew clothes by hand (bottom right).

INDUSTRIES: Mines and machinery are useless without men to run them, and such men are in short supply in parts of the Middle East. Some who do exist: Israeli phosphate miners (top left), a Saudi oil refinery mechanic (bottom left), and a Libyan explosives expert (below).

THE CULTURE

"Your religions can spring up only on dry land, very dry land, all rocks and pits and sand deserts and burning sun, except for an occasional terrific thunderstorm from nowhere," said U.S. writer George Santayana. Do you agree? How might sun and sand and thunderstorms affect religious beliefs?

*TRADITIONS: The Middle East has a
special sense of history, for it was here that
history began. Above, ancient temple carving
in Luxor, Egypt. Top right, timeless craft
of jewelry-making. Top far right, page from
Moslem holy book, the Koran. Bottom right,
Egyptians at cemetery near Giza pyramids.*

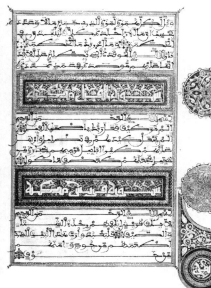

RELIGIONS: As the birthplace of three major religions, the Middle East contains many impressive houses of worship, like Istanbul's Hagia Sophia mosque (above). But Middle Easterners also worship in simple surroundings. In Jerusalem a Moslem prays in street as son waits (top left), while Jews gather to pray at ancient Wailing Wall.

LEARNING: In the past few years, the
chances for young Middle Easterners to get
an education have expanded greatly. Above,
Iranian women learn to read. Top right, children
in a Cairo nursery. Right, Israeli students in the
library at Jerusalem's Hebrew University.

3
PATTERNS
OF
CHANGE

Chapter 9

Turkey:
Astride Two Continents

LIKE MOST TURKISH TEENAGERS, Zeynep* is familiar with her country's glorious past. She's learned how the Turks once ruled a great empire stretching from the outskirts of Vienna to Baghdad, along the northern rim of Africa, and along the Red Sea coast of Arabia. She also knows that her country is no longer a world power, and yet she is proud of it.

This sort of national spirit has become a Turkish trademark. In part, it is a pride in the things which make Turkey different from its neighbors. To be sure, the Turks have much in common with other Middle Easterners, especially their Moslem faith. Nonetheless, Turkey has its own geography, history, and language. All this sets the Turks apart from other people of the Middle East.

One important difference is visible on a map of the Middle East. Turkey is located both in Asia and in Europe. Slicing through the country is a waterway called the Turkish Straits. The straits also divide Europe from Asia, leaving Turkey with one foot in the East and just a big toe in the West.

The "big toe" is Turkish Thrace, a spit of land about the size of Massachusetts. Though this area contains the city of Edirne and part of Istanbul,* it is otherwise sparsely populated. The "foot" is Asian Turkey, called Anatolia. Anatolia is 32 times larger than Turkish Thrace and holds 90 percent of Turkey's population.

Because it straddles two continents, Turkey is one of the world's most valuable pieces for real estate. For centuries it has played host to a wide array of peoples from all directions. First to come were the Hittites, warriors who swept in from central Asia about 3000 B.C. Over the years, others followed, including the Greeks and Romans.

Zeynep's father, who is a tour guide, enjoys taking his 15-year-old daughter to one of the sights he knows best: the ruins of the Greek settlement at Ephesus. Greeks first settled here in the 11th century B.C. and built a city of marble-paved roads and beautiful temples, including the spectacular Temple of Artemis, named for a goddess of nature. This temple was one of the Seven Wonders of the ancient world. Over a period of several hundred years, the city fell into ruins, and the ruins were buried by debris. Since the 1870's archeologists have been digging in the area to recover the ancient marvels. Today, most of the remains of Ephesus have been uncovered and restored to view.

The Greeks were fine architects, but the area's most important migrants came after them. In about the seventh and eighth centuries A.D., Turkish peoples from East Asia began moving west. Along the way they were converted to the new faith of Islam, and in the 11th century, they arrived in Anatolia and settled down.

In their adopted homeland the Turks built a fearsome reputation as fighters. One tribe in particular, the Ottomans, was clearly the most powerful. By the 1400's, the Ottomans had created an empire which

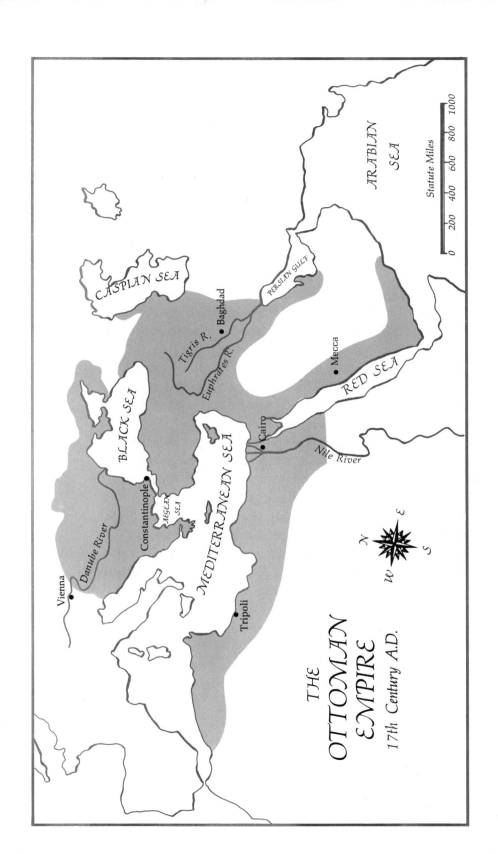

THE
OTTOMAN
EMPIRE
17th Century A.D.

Statute Miles
0   200   400   600   800   1000

ARABIAN SEA

CASPIAN SEA

PERSIAN GULF

Tigris R.   Baghdad

Euphrates R.

Mecca

RED SEA

BLACK SEA

Cairo

Nile River

MEDITERRANEAN SEA

AEGEAN SEA

Constantinople

Danube River

Vienna

Tripoli

N   E
W   S

stretched across the Middle East.

Why were the Ottomans so successful at empire-building? First, as Moslems they were eager to extend the kingdom of Allah. Second, they developed a skilled corps of shock troops made up of former prisoners of war. Thirdly, the Ottomans had a knack of making conquered people feel at home in the empire. All in all, the Ottomans were shrewd rulers.

The power of the Ottomans reached its peak in the 16th century under the rule of a sultan named Suleiman* the Magnificent. He dubbed himself "sultan of sultans, sovereign of sovereigns, dispenser of crowns to monarchs on the face of the earth." From Constantinople he ruled an empire that stretched from the outskirts of Vienna to Baghdad, along the northern rim of Africa, and down the Red Sea coast.

But even this mighty empire didn't last forever. In the 17th century, the Ottoman Empire began a slow but steady slide downhill. Its decline was due primarily to a failure to keep up with European science, and a failure to bring the army up-to-date. Branded the "sick man of Europe" in the 19th century, the Ottoman Empire resisted reform. The Turks seemed caught in the web of their own traditions. World War I dismantled the Empire, and modern Turkey was born.

Today, Turks like Zeynep wear Western style clothes, and call each other by Western style family names. Zeynep and her brother Hakan* live with their parents in the city of Izmir, a thriving port that was once a stopping-off along Asian caravan routes. The family's house is a two story stucco structure with a bright red tile roof.

Zeynep attends ninth grade at a school called Tugsa-

Turkey has been called a nation poised between past and future. What evidence is there to support or oppose this statement in this picture of Istanbul?

vul*. Like many other schools and streets in Turkey, Tugsavul is named after a military hero—in this case a former general in the Turkish army. In spite of the fact that Zeynep goes to classes six days a week, she considers herself very lucky. Before the 1920's Turkish women rarely went to school.

Zeynep and her family are devout Moslems. She wishes she had more time to practice her religion. Her mother still prays five times a day during the holy month of Ramadan. But other members of the family find it difficult to follow these rules, which conflict with school and work. What little free time they do have, they spend together. Their favorite family activity is going to the old marketplace.

In the old market Zeynep often gets the impression that time is standing still. Vendors push their vegetable carts through crowded walkways just as they have for centuries. Blacksmiths still hammer out farm tools in an unending shower of sparks. On especially hot days Zeynep purchases a cucumber and eats it to cool off. The vendor peels it for her so she can enjoy it while she shops.

Zeynep rarely goes to parties and never goes out on dates. Some of her older friends are allowed to do so, but Zeynep's parents think she's too young. In some parts of Turkey, girls, whose parents choose their husbands, get married at 15 or 16. But Zeynep thinks that's old-fashioned and her parents agree. Though she'll ask them to give their blessing in her marriage, she wants to choose her husband herself.

In the meantime, Zeynep has been planning a career. She loves small children, and she hopes to become a pediatrician (children's physician) some day. If she succeeds, she will be playing her part in the modernization of Turkey. Under Ottoman rule, most women would scarcely have thought of such a thing.

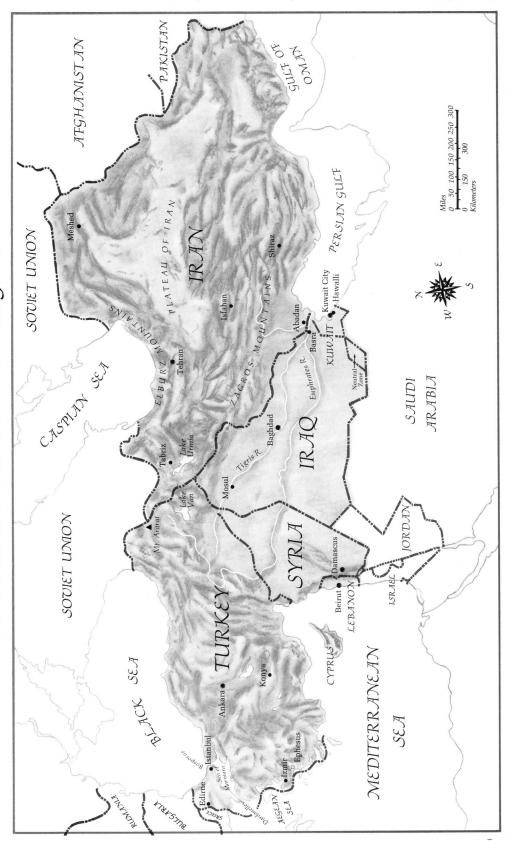

NORTHERN TIER AND NEIGHBORS

SOVIET UNION

AFGHANISTAN

PAKISTAN

GULF OF OMAN

Meshed

PLATEAU OF IRAN

IRAN

Shiraz

Isfahan

PERSIAN GULF

ELBURZ MOUNTAINS

Tehran

Abadan

Kuwait City

Hawalli

Basra

KUWAIT

ZAGROS MOUNTAINS

CASPIAN SEA

Neutral Zone

SOVIET UNION

Tabriz

Lake
Urmia

Euphrates R.

Baghdad

SAUDI
ARABIA

Lake
Van

Mosul

Tigris R.

IRAQ

Mt. Ararat

SYRIA

JORDAN

TURKEY

Damascus

Beirut

ISRAEL

BLACK SEA

Ankara

LEBANON

Konya

CYPRUS

MEDITERRANEAN
SEA

Istanbul

Sea of
Marmara

Bosporus

Edirne

Izmir

Ephesus

GREECE

Dardanelles

AEGEAN
SEA

BULGARIA

RUMANIA

Miles
0 50 100 150 200 250 300

0   150   300
Kilometers

N
W   E
S

*As modern Turkey's first president, Kemal Ataturk wore many
hats but shunned traditional Turkish headwear, the fez.*

FATHER
OF THE TURKS

HIS STEELY BLUE EYES, his high cheekbones, a brow
which wrinkled into ridges when he frowned — these features gave Mustafa Kemal* a determined look. And to his
fellow Turks he seemed their greatest leader. As president

of Turkey from 1923 to 1938, he picked up the pieces of a tottering, war-shattered country and fitted them into a modern nation.

At the time of Kemal's birth in 1881, Turkey did not even exist. It was then only a part of the Ottoman Empire which stretched eastward into Iraq and southward across North Africa into Libya.

On the day of his birth, Mustafa's father hung a sword on the wall above his cradle. The sword proved to be a sign of things to come. By the time Mustafa had entered his teens, he had decided to become a military man.

At the age of 12, he enrolled in a military school. There he turned out to be such a whiz at mathematics that his teacher named him "Kemal," which, in Arabic, means "perfection." At 18 he went on to a war college in Istanbul, the capital. In 1906 he entered the Ottoman army and swiftly rose through the ranks.

He was serving as a lieutenant colonel in 1914 when World War I broke across Europe. The Ottoman Empire quickly joined with Germany opposing the Allied forces which included Britain, France, and, later, the U.S. The fighting gave Kemal a chance to gain fame for his courage and leadership on the battlefield. But the war did not end happily for the Ottoman Empire, which went down to defeat in 1918.

With the end of the war, the empire collapsed into ruins. The Allied powers occupied the city of Istanbul, and the Greeks, with Allied aid, invaded other Ottoman areas. City and countryside fell into total chaos, and some Turks looked to the military as the only means of restoring order. All the while, many military officers talked openly of forming the Turkish people of the Ottoman Empire into one nation.

These officers needed leadership. Proud, ambitious Mustafa Kemal could offer it. In 1920 a National Congress met, and named Kemal president of a temporary government. In the next two years Kemal's influence spread steadily across his country. Finally, in 1923, he and his supporters created the Republic of Turkey.

Though Kemal claimed to be heading a democracy, he actually ruled with an iron hand. No sooner did he enter office than he started rebuilding Turkey — doing it from the ground up. Hospitals, roads, and power plants were built. New schools were constructed and staffed. A man who had always wanted "to be somebody" had become "somebody," and now he was getting something done.

Kemal enjoyed being powerful, but he always used his power to do what he thought best for his people. Perhaps his hardest job was breaking with many customs developed during the existence of the Ottoman Empire. Kemal lessened the influence of Islam in education and public affairs. He replaced Moslem holy laws with European laws. He urged that Turkish men doff their traditional fezzes in favor of Western hats. He tried to persuade Turkish women to remove their veils. He told them to stop "cringing like animals" when men looked at them in the streets.

One of Kemal's most important reforms — and one of his last — concerned the confusing matter of Turkish names. For centuries, Turks had followed the Arab practice of using only a given name and sometimes a father's name — Mahmud,* son of Ahmed, for instance. Trouble was, Turkey had a great many Mahmuds and Ahmeds, and it was sometimes difficult telling who was who.

So, in 1935, Kemal asked his countrymen to adopt family names in the Western manner — that is, Turkish counterparts to Smith and Jones. Kemal himself dropped his Arab name, Mustafa, and became known as Kemal Ataturk.* The new name meant "Kemal, Father of the Turks."

If another man had taken that name, it would have been a meaningless boast. For Ataturk, it was a simple statement of fact. More than anyone else, he had been responsible for the founding of modern Turkey. More than anyone else, he had kindled its spirit. When he died in 1938, he left behind a people both happier and healthier than he had found them. To this day Kemal Ataturk remains a Turkish hero without equal.

Double-check

Review

1. On what two continents is Turkey located?

2. Although Zeynep has to attend classes six days a week, she considers herself very lucky. Why?

3. Name two causes for the decline of the Ottoman Empire.

4. Who was modern Turkey's first president?

5. Kemal Ataturk replaced Moslem holy laws with what kind of laws?

Discussion

1. Do you think Turkey's geography and history have made the country more European or more Asian? Explain your answer.

2. In what ways, if any, would Turkey's recent history be different if Kemal Ataturk had not come into power? Using Kemal as your primary example, explain your answer to this question: "Do leaders create history, or does history create leaders?"

3. Why do you suppose Kemal Ataturk urged his people to drop their use of traditional dress and adopt Western dress? Do you think this was a reasonable request? Would you like the President of your country telling you how to dress? Explain your answer.

Activities

1. A group of students might develop a timeline of Turkish history from Greek or Roman times to the present. The timeline could be displayed in the classroom.

2. Some students might research and then draw pictures of Turkish costumes. The completed drawings could be put on a bulletin board under one of two headings: "Traditional Turkish Dress" and "Modern Turkish Dress."

3. The map on page 135 shows the Ottoman Empire to be extensive. Students might do research on other great empires — Alexander the Great's Empire, the Roman Empire, the British Empire — to discover how these empires were built and controlled, why they were not larger, and why they declined. In reports to the class, these empires could be compared with the Ottoman Empire.

Skills

Use the list below and information and maps in Chapters 5 and 9 to do the following on a separate sheet of paper.

Each of the numbered phrases describes the Arab Empire, the Ottoman Empire, or both. For each item, write "A" if the item describes the Arab Empire, "B" if the item describes the Ottoman Empire, or "A and B" if the item describes both empires.

A THE ARAB EMPIRE

B THE OTTOMAN EMPIRE

1. The larger empire.

2. The empire of the eighth century A.D.

3. Included Constantinople.

4. Founded by the Turks.

5. Followers of Islam.

6. Opposed the Allied forces.

7. Baghdad was the capital.

8. The later of the empires.

9. Founded by Arab tribes.

10. Ruled by Suleiman the Magnificent.

11. Conquered Jerusalem in 638 A.D.

12. Led by Omar.

13. Defeated at the Battle of Tours.

14. Termed "the sick man of Europe."

15. Spread the Arabic language across the Middle East.

16. Its scholars translated the ancient Greeks.

Chapter 10

Saudi Arabia:

High-Tech Kingdom

FIFTY YEARS AGO MOST of Saudi Arabia was vast, untouched desert. The only inhabitants were tribes of nomads who traveled, as they had for centuries, across the sands on sturdy, but slow-moving camels. Today, cars and trucks speed along the superhighways that crisscross Saudi Arabia's desert. Saudi Arabia has leapt from medieval times to the modern age in one generation.

What's behind this giant leap forward? Oil. Oil was discovered under Saudi deserts in 1939, and today Saudi Arabia is the third largest oil producer in the world. (Only the U.S. and the U.S.S.R. produce more.) The income from the oil has changed the once impoverished desert land into a nation of sleek, modern cities and hi-tech industry.

Even teenagers can remember when their country was different. Mawada, who is 16, lives in the city of Jeddah. She recalls the time when Jeddah was a town

Saudi Arabian men gather around a modern fountain in present-day Mecca. As one can see, much of this area is being rebuilt.

with a few paved streets and nowhere to go. Now it is home for a million people. Like most Saudi Arabian cities, it has skyscrapers, shopping centers, supermarkets, and fast-food restaurants.

But for all it's modern ways. Saudi Arabia is still a very traditional country. All political power is in the hands of the royal family, the house of Saud. The family members chose a king from among themselves. Today, King Fahd Ibn Abdul-Aziz al-Saud is the head of the family and the country's supreme religious leader. His brother, Crown Prince Abdullah, is the prime minister. The laws of the country come from the teachings of the Islamic religion.

The royal family is descended from Ibn Saud, who as a powerful young leader in the early 1900's unified the nomadic tribes of the Arabian peninsula. These tribes had been warring for centuries. Unification took 30 years, but in 1939 Ibn Saud declared himself king and named the country Saudi Arabia.

Saud's kingdom was huge, but virtually penniless. So meager was the government's treasury that it could be carried around in a single trunk. Riches only came with the discovery of oil. Many top Saudi leaders remember their country's poor past, and want to insure that the oil wealth is spent wisely.

For that reason education is a top priority in Saudi Arabia. Crewmen on the oil tankers that regularly travel up and down the Persian Gulf can pinpoint their location by a gleaming tower that rises from a high point on the edge of the Saudi Arabian desert. The lighted tower is the beacon for a university built by oil, for oil, and about oil. Saudi Arabia's University of Petroleum and Minerals is only 20 years old. But it is already a center for advanced engineering studies in the Middle East.

Despite the bleak desert location (daytime temperatures sometimes reach 115 degrees Fahrenheit) the university is not a bad place to study. There is no tuition for the Moslem students who come from 19 countries. In fact, the Saudi Arabian government gives each student a monthly allowance for living expenses. Students have the use of 13 tennis courts, four soccer fields, and an Olympic-sized swimming pool. But they still cannot ignore the desert. Most students wear the traditional white desert robes outdoors. These robes are good protection against the heat and the desert sandstorms that sometimes blow across the campus.

The university is just one example of the Saudi Arabia's commitment to education. Between 1978 and 1983, a new elementary or secondary school opened every three weeks somewhere in the nation. Education is completely free for all students. This has meant a population explosion in Saudi schools. In the 1950's, only about 10,000 young people—all boys—attended school. Now there are over 850,000 young people in Saudi Arabian schools, and 43 percent of them are girls.

Najeba* is a high school student in the city of Riyadh.* She wears a floor-length gray uniform to school. On the street she is heavily veiled. Inside the all-female school, however, Najeba and her classmates always remove their veils. All the men in Najeba's family, even her 17-year-old brother, own cars. Gasoline prices are very low, so running a car is no problem. But Najeba does not own a car, or even drive one. Women are not allowed to drive cars in Saudi Arabia.

In other ways, too, Saudi Arabia is a country where modern practices and traditional ideas coexist. Business and development are officially encouraged by the government, and Saudi Arabia has experienced an industrial boom in recent years. However, Saudi factories, markets, and offices still come to a standstill five times a day as workers stop for prayers. The call-to-prayer

King Faisal, who died in 1976, walks to a Muslin place of worship
surrounded by his followers. Like millions of Muslims all over
the world, the king prayed five times a day.

✑ Mawada will never own a car. Saudi Arabian women are not allowed to drive.

chant resounds from the mosques and the population turns toward Mecca, the Moslem holy city, to pray.

Saudi Arabians like to tell a story about their nation's first telephone system which was installed years ago, in the time of Ibn Saud. Religious leaders were doubtful about this new-fangled gadget. But the king demonstrated the telephone by reading into it selections from the Koran, the Moslem holy book. This convinced the religious leaders that the telephone was acceptable. They reasoned that anything that carried the word of Allah could not be bad.

Saudi religious customs sometimes startle foreigners. Mawada, who has visited the U.S. twice, says, "Americans used to stare at my clothes. In public all Saudi women, for religious reasons, wear long-sleeved dresses, a scarf, and a full-length cape called an *abaya.* Many women also wear the veil." Saudi men generally wear an ankle-length white shirt called a *throbe,* which may be covered with by a robe, jacket or cloak. On their heads they wear a *keffiyah,** a piece of cloth held in place by a rope band. This provides protection against the sun and wind.

In general, Saudi Arabians tend to be very private people. They prefer to live with their families, including members of several generations, in homes surrounded by high walls. The government has recently built many high-rise apartment complexes in major cities, but most Saudis who can afford it buy private homes. The government gives them interest-free loans for this.

Mawada's family lives in an apartment, which she

considers small but cozy. It has three bedrooms, a kitchen, a dining room, and two living rooms. One living room is for women and the other for men. When guests come and the men and women are strangers, they sit apart. But the family sits together when they are alone. "When my father comes home from work, we sit with him and drink tea, and sometimes watch TV. It's very nice," Mawada says.

Mawada is proud of her country, especially the way it has managed to mix the old and the new. She points out that every year Saudi Arabia is using technology to improve life for its citizens. Once the country had to import most of its food. Today, thanks to new irrigation projects and scientific farming methods, the country has enough wheat to feed its own people, and some left over to export. "We're taking many steps forward, but we aren't forgetting the past and our traditions. That makes me glad," Mawada says.

Double-check

Review

1. In the last 50 years Saudi Arabia has become a rich country. Why?

2. Who was Ibn Saud? What did he do for Saudi Arabia?

3. If Mawada had been born 50 years ago, how might her life be different?

4. What is one of the highest priorities of Saudi Arabia's government?

5. What is a *keffiyah*?

Discussion

1. What does the story of Saudi Arabia's first telephone tell you about the way Saudi Arabians have adapted to modernization?

2. Is the title of the chapter "High-Tech Kingdom" a good way to describe Saudi Arabia? In what ways is the country modern? In what ways is it traditional?

3. Why do you think Mawada is proud of the way her country has changed? Does her thinking make sense to you? Would you find the kind of restrictions she lives unacceptable? If so, why do you think she feels so in harmony with her world?

Activities

1. Saudi Arabia is a close ally of the United States, one of closest of the Arab nations. Some students might research the history of this alliance. Why is it so close? How have the two countries helped each other in the past?

2. Students might produce an imaginary travelogue, pretending they have recently visited Saudi Arabia and their job is now to entice others to go there.

3. Have a Saudi Arabian day. Students could dress in Saudi costumes and prepare traditional Saudi dishes. To learn more about the cuisine and costumes of the Saudis, students might research in books, encyclopedia, and magazines. They could also write to the Saudi embassy in Washington.

Skills

WORLD TRADE IN SOME
MIDDLE EASTERN COUNTRIES, 1986

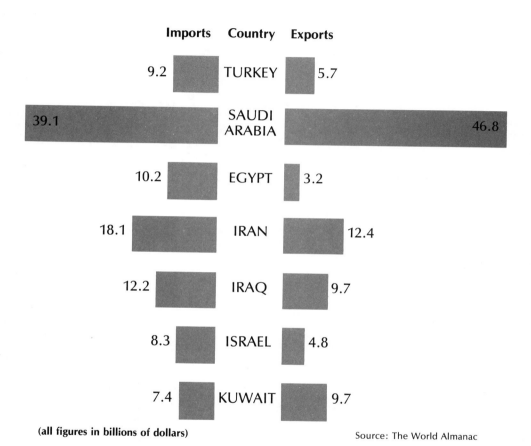

Imports   Country   Exports

	Country	
9.2	TURKEY	5.7
39.1	SAUDI ARABIA	46.8
10.2	EGYPT	3.2
18.1	IRAN	12.4
12.2	IRAQ	9.7
8.3	ISRAEL	4.8
7.4	KUWAIT	9.7

(all figures in billions of dollars)

Source: The World Almanac

Use the bar graph above and information in Chapter 10 to answer the following questions.

1. What do the numbers on the left represent?

2. What was the value of all Israeli exports in 1983?

3. Which country had the greatest dollar value of imports in 1983?

4. Which country had the greatest dollar value of exports in 1983?

5. How many countries import more than they export?

Chapter 11

Kuwait:
Rags to Riches

THERE WERE ONLY a few great cities in the old Middle East — among them: Baghdad, Damascus, Mecca, Fez, and Cairo. For every great city, however, there were hundreds of ordinary small towns. Some were market towns where the Bedouins or the local fellahin came to trade. Others were oasis towns where caravans stopped for water and supplies on their way across the desert. Still others were port towns where goods passed in and out of the country, and where the overland caravan routes began.

One such small town, a port town, grew up on the shores of a deep bay on the eastern coast of the Arabian Peninsula, in the northwestern part of the Persian Gulf. The land around the bay was called Kuwait. It belonged to desert people, called Kuwaitis, who had long ago come to the area from central Arabia and decided to settle down.

The sea was the most important influence in the

lives of the Kuwaitis. Many Kuwaitis became prosperous merchants and traders. Others were fishermen, pearl divers, sailors, longshoremen, or shipbuilders. Yet the people also lived on the edge of the desert. All the land around the bay was barren sand.

Like much of the Arabian Peninsula, Kuwait was very dry. So drinking water for the townspeople had to be imported — shipped daily down the Persian Gulf from Iraq. The sea provided fish, and there were a few small oasis areas. But outside these areas there were no trees, not even date palms. Except for the fast-fading flowers which blossomed in the desert after the winter rains, hardly a green thing grew anywhere. Like its water, almost all of Kuwait's food had to be imported.

Kuwait was typical of Arabian Peninsula lands in another way: time seemed to bring hardly any change at all. Unlike Egypt, for example, Kuwait had no ancient monuments to attract tourists. Until the 1930's, only a handful of Westerners had ever been in Kuwait. Even fewer Kuwaitis knew anything about the world outside their little homeland.

In the center of the town was a big open market. There herdsmen and tradesmen spread their wares on the ground, and Bedouins brought their camels and sheep to sell. Bedouins could always be seen in Kuwait town, for several tribes roamed the Kuwaiti deserts.

At night the streets of the town were dark. As late as 1940 the houses had no electricity. There were only three or four schools and one hospital. A wall surrounded the whole town, and the wall gates were locked each evening after nightfall. Beyond the wall was nothing but desert.

Except for a few tiny villages, and miles and miles of desert, that town was all that Kuwait had. Surely,

155

Rich Kuwaitis now use autos instead of mules as their "beasts of burden." But many men and women still dress in traditional Arab robes.

of all the Middle Eastern countries, Kuwait seemed just about the last that would ever change. But change came suddenly in the 1940's, bringing undreamed-of wealth and luxury to Kuwait. It was as though a real Aladdin had rubbed his lamp over this tiny desert land.

☆ ☆ ☆ ☆ ☆ ☆ ☆ ☆ ☆

When Ali's father, Bashar,* tells him about the old days in Kuwait, Ali can hardly believe it.

Ali is 14, and he never saw the old town on the bay. By the time he was born, it was much changed, and soon afterward it had all but vanished. The Kuwait that Ali knows has wide avenues crowded with cars and brightly lit at night. It has glass-fronted

156

office buildings, lavish homes, luxurious hotels, and an international jet airport. It has modern shops, and a main thoroughfare — lined with offices, hotels, and department stores — which runs through the middle of the city.

There are parks, too, filled with flowers and shrubs. These are set in the middle of traffic circles or alongside schools and other public buildings. There are many tree-lined avenues. It costs much money to make green things grow in a desert land like Kuwait. Each day trucks must bring the necessary water to each park and each tree.

But the *emir*,* or ruler, of the country is richer now than all the great caliphs of Baghdad put together ever were or ever hoped to be. His people have more than enough money to buy equipment which can turn brackish water, once useless to them, into water fresh enough for growing plants. They don't wait anxiously for ships carrying water from Iraq any more — they "make" their own drinking water instead. Each day millions of gallons of salty water are pumped into a huge new plant. In this plant the water is purified, and the salt and other minerals are removed.

Kuwait has so much money that no one there has to be poor. If anybody needs a house, the Kuwaiti government either builds him one at low cost, lends him the money to build one himself, or rents him one for as little as three dollars a month. If anybody needs a job, the government trains him for one, free, or lends him the money to start a business of his own and then helps him to run it. If anybody, even with all this help, still cannot properly support his family, the government pays him, monthly, the extra money he needs.

There are hospitals of many kinds in Kuwait, and all of them are free. There are more than 300 schools ranging from kindergarten to Kuwait University, and these are free, too. If Kuwaiti girls and boys choose to, they may go to almost any college or university in the world, and the Kuwaiti government pays their tuition and travel costs, and gives them money for living expenses. People who are sick can get the medical care they need, free, even if they must be sent to another country to get it. There are no taxes in Kuwait — the government doesn't need the money.

Kuwait has more doctors for each 1,000 of its people than many other nations have. Almost every family in Kuwait owns a car, and many have more than one. There are well over 200 mosques in the country, most of them new. Beautiful villas and palaces built by members of the emir's family stand in once-lonely desert areas.

How could Kuwait become so rich, and in such a short time? How could a land which had not changed for centuries become, in just a few years, probably the most modern country in the Middle East?

The answer: oil.

Even before 1940, British and American oilmen knew there was oil under Kuwait's sand. World War II put a stop to drilling, however. As soon as the war was over in 1945, more test wells were dug. By 1954, Kuwait earned about 200 million dollars a year from oil. Twenty-five years later, it earned about 11 billion dollars. Money like this goes a long way in a country with under two million people, half of whom aren't even Kuwaitis. They have moved to Kuwait from all over the Middle East looking for jobs.

Ali and his family live about four miles southeast of Kuwait city, in the town of Hawalli.* Once almost everything beyond the city walls was barren desert. Now many modern towns like Hawalli have grown up to the east, south, and west of the capital. Each

158

Thirty-five years ago Kuwait had less than five schools. Now every student has a chance to attend school for at least eight years.

has its medical clinic, shopping center, schools, theaters, parks, and mosques. Modern highways link the towns with one another and with Kuwait City.

The house in which Ali lives was built in 1958. Like the old Kuwaiti houses, it has a flat roof and is surrounded by high walls. In almost every other way it is Western. It is two stories high and modern in design, with wide windows, a balcony on the upper floor, and a small front garden. The walls are of white concrete, trimmed in bright pink. The house is roomy enough for the whole family: Ali's grandparents, parents, and two sisters.

159

Inside, Ali's house is air-conditioned, as are almost all buildings in Kuwait. It has a modern kitchen and a telephone, and most of its furniture is Western in style. But the family has set aside one room for mostly traditional furnishings such as floor cushions and low tables. In that room the family usually relaxes while sitting around the television set.

On the roof of the house is a storage tank for the family's drinking and cooking water. The water is delivered regularly by truck, pumped into the roof tank, and piped from there into the house.

Ali's family pays much more for every gallon of fresh water they use than do families in the United States. But making salt water drinkable is a very expensive process.

Ali doesn't remember his grandfather's run-down old house in Kuwait City. He was only four years old when the family moved to Hawalli. But the grandfather tells him about it, and Ali has seen houses like it. A few are still left, wedged in between the new buildings, in the oldest parts of the city. Hardly anyone lives in these old houses any more. After 1950, when Kuwait began to earn a lot of money from oil, most people were able to build new homes.

Like many Kuwaitis, Ali's family got the money to build their new house by selling their old one to the government. The emir decided that a good way to share the new oil wealth with the people was to buy at high prices all of the property they were willing to sell. The government needed the land for new buildings and streets. No matter how old or poor a house or shop might be, or how tiny or worthless a plot of land, the owners were sure to receive a good deal of money for it. People who had always been poor suddenly became rich, and families who had always owned much property, but little else, became millionaires.

Double-check

Review

1. The shores of Kuwait are on what gulf?

2. What is an emir?

3. Who pays the costs of university and college education for Kuwaiti students?

4. What has made Kuwait such a wealthy country?

5. Why is there a storage tank on the roof of Ali's house?

Discussion

1. Because the government of Kuwait is so wealthy, it provides free medical care, jobs, low-cost housing, and other benefits for its citizens. Do you think the United States government could or should do the same for all Americans? Why, or why not? To what extent does the United States government provide these things for Americans? Why?

2. How do the ways Kuwaitis and Americans obtain and use water differ? Do you think the Kuwaitis are justified in using their water on parks, flowers, and trees? How would your life be different if you had to pay a much higher price for water?

3. Do you think Kuwait would have a hard time defending itself against a larger country that wanted to seize control of its oil resources? Why, or why not? How have small countries defended themselves in the past? What means might Kuwait use to defend itself?

Activities

1. Some students might draw pictures of what they think the town of Kuwait looked like before the 1940's. Then you could obtain photographs of the modern city of Kuwait and put the contrasting visuals on a bulletin board.

2. Some students might be interested in researching and giving an oral presentation on one of the following processes: (a) desalinizing water; (b) exploring for oil; (c) extracting and refining oil.

3. The Southwestern United States has had water shortages in past years. Students could collect articles and pictures on how water is used in the Southwest and on what efforts are being made to conserve water there. Several students might report to the class on their findings.

Skills

POPULATION MAKEUP

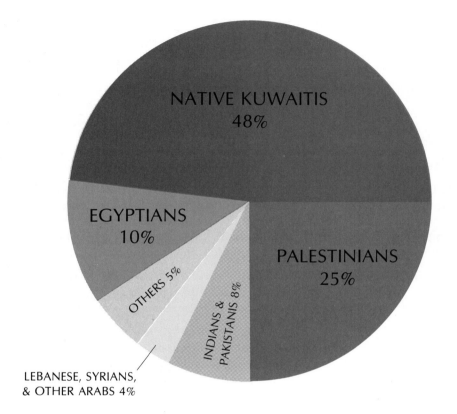

LEBANESE, SYRIANS,
& OTHER ARABS 4%

Use the circle graph above and information in Chapter 11 to answer the following questions.

1. What are the two major population groups in Kuwait?

2. What percentage of Kuwait's population is Egyptian?

3. Do native Kuwaitis make up more or less than half of the total population?

4. An American now living in Kuwait would be included in which population group?

5. Which group in the graph probably, before the 1930's, made up a larger percentage of the population than it does now?

Chapter 12

Militant Islam

ONE NIGHT IN OCTOBER 1983, an explosive-packed truck crashed thorugh the gates of a United States barracks in Beirut, Lebanon. It blew up, killing 241 sleeping Marines. Soon after, a terrorist group claimed credit for the raid. A spokesperson declared the group had committed the raid in the name of God. Then, members hailed the truck's suicide driver as a saint.

What was the motive for this attack? Why would a religious group plan and carry out such a brutal slaying? Could such attacks be prevented in future? Those questions obsessed experts, and the world, at the time.

Now it is known that the bombing was the work of Islamic extremists. Such extremists have been behind numerous other terrorist incidents around the world in recent years. Each group of extremists has its own particular motives, but experts believe they all have something in common. They are part of a movement sweeping the Middle East which is called militant Islam.

Even young children are sometimes involved in the militant Islam movement. These boys in Iran are taking part in a protest parade. They wear headbands declaring their faith and commitment to Allah.

Militant means aggressive or fighting. Militant Islamics are fighting for their faith. Many feel that the modern world has led Moslems too far away from the ancient practices of their religion. They seek a return to tradition in dress, prayer, diet, and behavior all over the Moslem world. Militant Islam has political goals, as well, related the return to a truer faith. It is in pursuit of these political goals that many militants turn to terrorism.

Who do militant Islamics oppose? Above all they are against people or nations they believe weaken the traditions of Islam. Many believe that through the increasing contacts between Arab and Western nations, the U.S. included, Moslems are learning new ways rather than following the old. Militants want to reverse this trend. So they strike out against the West where they can, such as in Beirut at the Marine barracks.

The United States is also a favorite target because it is an ally of Israel. Israel occupies land many Moslems regard as rightfully Arab and Moslem. Militants vigorously oppose anyone willing to recognize Israel. Even Arab nations or leaders who deal with Israel can be targets for Islamic militants. In 1981, Egypt's President Anwar Sadat was gunned down by militants. Sadat had signed a peace treaty with Israel two years before.

Nowhere is militant Islam stronger than in Iran. That nation is headed by a religious leader, the Ayatollah Ruhollah Khomeini, whose supporters overthrew the U.S.-backed Shah Mohammed Reza Pahlevi in 1979. Under the Ayatollah, Iran has fought a long, bloody war against neighboring Iraq. Iraq is far richer in arms and resources than Iran. Iranians call the war a *jihad,* meaning holy crusade. Experts believe that Iran has been able to continue fighting despite great hardship because of the devotion the Ayatollah commands.

This devotion can be frightening. Iranian volunteers

aged 12 to 17 have been sent into battle against the Iraqis with little to defend themselves. According to some reports, young soldiers are roped together to keep them from deserting as others are blown into the air by land mines. All the soldiers carry small metal keys to Paradise. The Ayatollah's followers are convinced that if they die a martyr's death on the battlefield, they will be transported instantly to the gates of heaven. Indeed, Iranian leaders have taught young people that it is their duty and their fate to sacrifice their lives to further the spread of Islam.

The obsession with martyrdom is found in other countries of the Middle East, too. Suicide bombings, such as that at the Marine barracks, have become common in Lebanon. These attacks require a terrorist to drive a vehicle laden with explosives into a targeted building to be blown up along with the cargo. Most volunteers for these suicide missions are under 21 years of age. According to experts these young people turn to self-destruction out of religious passion and hate. Lebanon has been torn by civil war for over a decade, and many teens there have known nothing but poverty and violence. This makes them willing to strike out at those they perceive as their enemies.

In general, experts believe that militant Islam is a response to modernization. The rush of the Middle East to catch up with the West brings numerous changes. These changes are unsettling to many. Militant Islam also has strong roots in the past. There is an Islamic tradition of action, militancy, and martyrdom.

Mohammed, the prophet who established Islam, preached that to simply believe in the teachings of the religion was not enough. A Moslem must promote justice among others through his own actions. This is one of the most basic tenets of Islam.

After Mohammed died, Moslems quarreled over who

would succeed him as political leader of the Islamic world. The majority agreed that Abu Bakr, a long-time associate of the prophet should be the new leader. But a minority believed that Ali, Mohammed's son-in-law, was the prophet's rightful heir. This minority set out to overthrow Abu Bakr in order, they said, to restore justice and truth.

The civil war between Abu Bakr's supporters, called the Sunnis, and Ali's, called the Shiites, lasted 30 years. In one battle, Mohammed's grandson Husayn stormed a Sunni stronghold and was killed. Shiites consider Husayn the supreme martyr. Every year on the holy day of Ashura, they reenact his death.

Most of today's militant Islamics are Shiites. They are carrying on the tradition which calls martyrdom the most honorable defense of the faith. The Shiites lost the civil war, and only in one country, Iran, are they the majority of citizens. And yet, they play an important role on the world stage. The urge that led Shiites to try to topple the Moslem leadership in the seventh century has a new target: foreign influence. Today they fight to preserve their faith against the ideas and customs of the non-believers. Unfortunately, their fight all too often involves innocent people.

Libya's leader Muammer Gaddafi preachs the age-old dream of Arab unity.

THE QUEST FOR UNITY

AGAIN AND AGAIN in this century, the force of nationalism has crackled like lightening across the non-Western world. Wherever it's gone, it has made a big difference in the way people think about themselves. Nationalism is basically the wish for national unity and independence by people who share similiar languages and customs. Nowhere has this wish been more evident than in the Arab world.

The story of Arab nationalism really begins with another "ism" —colonialism. Colonialism in the Middle East amounted to long centuries of foreign rule. From the 16th century to the 19th, much of the area was part of the Ottoman Empire and was ruled from Istanbul. Then, as Ottoman power declined in the 19th century, several European powers gobbled up large hunks of Middle Eastern territory.

Starting in the 1840's, France grabbed vast sections of North Africa. Not to be outdone, Britain occupied Egypt, and Italy occupied Libya. After World War I, France took control in Lebanon and Syria, and Britain in Palestine and Jordan. The only major area ignored by Europeans was Saudi Arabia.

European colonialism did have its benefits. One of them was modernization—the building of roads, irrigation projects and telegraph lines in many different areas and the development of industries based on Middle Eastern oil.

But as time went on, European control chaffed the Arabs' pride. "Why can't we govern ourselves?" Arabs asked each other. They staged demonstrations to back up their demands for self-government.

Nationalism was on the rise, but not all of it sprang from hatred of the Europeans. Often the movement was also inspired by a look backward. A world which had once been united by leaders such as Mohammed and Omar could be united again—or so many Arabs believed. The first step, they thought, was to throw off the shackles of European control.

Their quest for independence bore fruit in Syria, Lebanon, and Libya immediately after World War II. In Syria and Lebanon uprisings finally forced the French to leave in 1946. Libyan independence was set in motion by Italy's defeat in World War II. The United Nations granted Libya self-rule in 1951.

But sometimes winning independence wasn't so easy. Two cases in point:

Algeria. In the course of a century of colonial rule, many French settled in Algeria where they set down deep roots. They considered the colony a part of France. But this seemed absurd to Moslem Algerians, who outnumbered European Algerians by 10 to one.

In 1954 Moslem discontent flared into open war. For five years both sides battled with brutal fury. Finally French President Charles de Gaulle said that he would give Algerians the right to decide if they wanted to remain linked to France or not. In 1962 Algerians voted overwhelmingly for independence.

Egypt. Angry outbursts against Europeans were also common here. Only in this case the Europeans were the British who took control of Egypt in 1882. In time Arab rioting forced Britain to ease its control. In 1922 Britain made Egypt an independent monarchy. Still the British continued to control the king's treasury and his foreign affairs. Thus nationalists considered their so-called independence a sham.

After World War II more and more Egyptians denounced their government as corrupt and unwilling to make reforms. In 1952 their protests overflowed into revolution. Egyptian military officers took control of the government, and the king was driven into exile.

A key figure in this revolution was a young army colonel named Gamal Abdel Nasser. While still a student at military academy, Nasser formed a Free Officers Movement composed of fellow nationalists his own age. That organization was a major force behind the 1952 revolution.

In 1954 Nasser seized the reins of the revolution he had helped to start. One of his first tasks was to persuade the British to remove their remaining troops in Egypt. The British signed an agreement to that effect in July 1954. Then Nasser got down to the most important business of reform—building Egyptian industries and breaking up the huge estates owned by a small group of wealthy landowners.

Over the years Nasser established himself as a daring politician and a spellbinding speaker. As his reputation grew, he became the spokesman for the Arab nationalist cause. In Nasser, the Arab nations had a forceful leader.

Reuniting the Arab world became Nasser's great dream. In January 1958 he succeeded in forging a union of Egypt and Syria into the United Arab Republic (UAR). This seemed the first big step in unifying the Arab world. But it didn't work. In 1961 Syria withdrew over political differences with Nasser. In the last years of his life, Nasser continued to promote his ideal of Arab unity. He died in 1970 without seeing it realized.

But the dream of Arab unity did not die with Nasser. Today several Arab leaders claim to be heir to Nasser's legacy. Most notable among them is Colonel Muammer Gaddafi, leader of Libya. Like Nasser, Gaddafi was trained in military schools and led a coup to overthrow his country's king in 1969. Since then, Gaddafi has modernized and reformed life in Libya. He's used oil revenues to pay for free housing, medical care, and education for all Libyans.

Gaddafi says he intends to do more, outside the borders of Libya. In his frequent public speeches he constantly lectures other Arab nations on the need for a united front against the West. He says Arabs have been humiliated for centuries and only a new Arab empire under his leadership can reverse that trend. Gaddafi has formed union with Egypt, Morocco, Syria and Sudan. But these unions have all proved to be worth little more than the paper they are printed on. The differences between the nations are too great for much cooperative action.

Gaddafi also supports terrorists who strike out at the West. This has gotten him into trouble with the United States, Britain, and France. Gaddafi defends his policies by saying the great Islamic empire will never be formed without violence. In this respect, Gaddafi is not only a nationalist, but part of the militant Islamic movement as well.

Gaddafi fanaticism, and the natural divisions in the Arab world may mean his dream of an Arab empire will always be simply that, a dream. Meanwhile, Arab nations are conscious of what they have in common. Most meet regularly to discuss problems and to carry out joint programs.

Double-check

Review

1. What does the term *militant Islam* mean?

2. In what country is militant Islam strongest?

3. Why is the U.S. a target for Islamic militants?

4. In the 1950's and 1960's who was the leading spokesman for the Arab nationalist cause?

5. In what ways does Gaddafi embody both militant Islam and Arab nationalism?

Discussion

1. Do you see Arab nationalism as a positive or negative movement? How could it help Arabs? How could it not help them? Why do you think the dream of Arab unity has not been realized? What kind of leader, or events would it take for the "dream" to come true?

2. Why do you think militant Islam is such a powerful force in the Middle East today? What makes people turn to violence to protect their traditions? Can you imagine a similar movement staring in the U.S.? Why, or why not?

3. Terrorism is a serious concern in the world today. While not all terrorists are Islamic militants, many of those that attack Americans are. What is the proper response to terrorist incidents? Can the U.S. government do anything to prevent such incidents over the long-term? In what ways could understanding and addressing the concerns of militant Islamics keep them from turning to terrorism? Do you think militant Islamics will continue to use terrorism to further their goals?

Activities

1. Some students might research and prepare reports on the current leaders of some Middle Eastern countries, covering such subjects as the leaders' childhoods, how they rose to power, how they view relations with the United States and how they feel about Arab unity.

2. Some students might draw a map of the Middle East showing which European countries at one time controlled territory there and when each Middle Eastern country obtained its independence.

3. A committee might clip newspapers and magazine articles, political cartoons and photographs concerning militant Islam and assemble a bulletin board display on the subject.

Skills

ROTHCO

Use the political cartoon above and information in Chapter 12 to answer the following questions.

1. In what Middle Eastern country is the action of this cartoon supposed to take place?

(a)Israel   (b)Lebanon   (c)Iraq

2. Who are the men driving the trucks?

(a) militant Islamics   (b) Russian spies   (c) goat farmers

3. Why are the men carrying TNT in their trucks?

(a) they want to make a terrorist attack against the West   (b) they feed it to their goats   (c) it's a gift for their mothers

4. What seems to be the main point of this cartoon?

(a) goats eat strange foods   (b) Middle Easterners are very polite   (c) terrorism is just a normal daily activity in Lebanon

173

4
ISRAEL

Chapter 13

Israel: Modern Ancient Land

"THE DESERT SHALL REJOICE," said a Biblical prophet about 700 B.C., "and blossom as the rose." Twenty-seven centuries later, in the land of Israel, the ancient prophesy is coming true. A bright green patchwork of fields and orchards is crowding out the yellow sand and brown rock of the Israeli desert.

Forty years ago, the land was very different. Except for a fertile strip along the Mediterranean coast, much of the area was considered too dry and rocky for farming. The hills of Judah, in the center, were badly eroded. Near Lake Tiberias (the ancient Sea of Galilee) were brackish swamps. The Dead Sea was so salty that no fish could live in it. And the Negev Desert in the south was as bleak and lifeless as the surface of the moon.

Yet today the Israeli people produce about three quarters of their own food and, in addition, export some. Since Israel's founding in 1948, the amount of food grown in Israel has increased six times. The Israelis have accomplished this by a combination of hard work and modern methods. Where the soil was dry, they irrigated it. Where swamps made the fields too wet for farming, they drained them.

All this activity took place in a startlingly tiny country. Israel rims the Mediterranean Sea for only about 150 miles from north to south, less than the distance from New York to Boston. From east to west, Israel's borders are about 70 miles wide at their widest point. That is less than an hour-and-a-half's drive on a U.S. superhighway.

Unlike most Middle Easterners, the people of Israel are primarily city dwellers. There are Israeli cities which are thousands of years old, such as Jerusalem, the capital; Hebron*; Jaffa*; Beersheba*; Caesarea*; Acre*; Tiberias*; and the port of Haifa.* And there are cities which are new, started since World War I or in the years since the founding of Israel. Railroads and highways crisscross much of the land. The houses have electricity. The country is prosperous.

David, 15, and his sister, Sarah, 10, live in one of the most modern parts of this modern land. Their home is in Tel Aviv,* the largest city in Israel. It is one of the country's new cities, started in 1909. Next to it is one of the oldest cities in the world, Jaffa. People consider these two cities, which lie side by side, as one—Tel Aviv-Jaffa.

Tel Aviv is sunny most of the time—warm in summer and never much colder than 50 or 60 degrees Fahrenheit in winter. (This is true of much of Israel. Except for the Negev, Israel has a pleasant climate.) The city faces on the Mediterranean Sea and has a fine beach.

Israeli farmers rely heavily on irrigation ditches to make their fruit trees thrive.

"The desert shall rejoice, and blossom as the rose."

It is usually crowded with tourists and Israelis. Almost everyone wears Western clothes. Cars, buses, taxis, and bicycles jam the streets. The beach is lined with large hotels, and the town has many museums, theaters, restaurants, and concert halls.

Tel Aviv is a center of business and commerce. About half of Israel's business and industry is carried on there. Many Tel Aviv residents, however, are suburbanites. They have houses in the hills to the north, and commute to work in the city. David and Sarah live in one of these suburbs. Their father is a journalist at a Tel Aviv newspaper.

The family's house is one story high and has five rooms, a porch, and a garden. This house is fairly large for Israel, where most houses have no more than three or four rooms. The walls are concrete, painted white. Wood is scarce, as it is in most other Middle Eastern countries, and most building is done in concrete, cement or stone, with stone floors. The house is furnished like ones in Europe or the U.S.

There are two things David's family doesn't have: a TV set and a car. These items are expensive in Israel— they cost about three times as much as in the United States.

David and Sarah were both born in Israel. But about a half of the citizens of Israel come from other lands. Many are Jews from the Arab countries of the Middle East. Many are from Europe. A few come from America. An important Israeli law says "Every Jew has the right to come to this country as settler."

Joseph and Anna, David and Sarah's parents, were born in Poland. Joseph was still a toddler when World War II began in 1939. Two years before, his family, like Anna's, had moved to Britain. They were lucky. During the war, all Joseph's uncles, aunts and cousins died in Nazi concentration camps.

In Britain, Joseph and Anna met and were married. They then went to live in Israel, which has been founded only 10 years before in 1948. During Isreal's early years, many European-born Jews immigrated there.

Abraham, who goes to high school with David, was born in Morocco. His father used to own a small shop in Fez. Then years ago, when Abraham was small, the family decided to come to Israel. Because they were used to city life, the family settled in happily in Tel Aviv.

Non-Jews also live in Israel. About 15 percent of the 4 million residents of Israel are Arabs. Most are Moslems, but there are small groups of Arab Christians as well. Israeli Arabs have full rights of citizenship in Israel. However, the Arabs who live on the West Bank, an area occupied by Israel since 1967, do not have such rights. (For more on the history and the problems of the West Bank see Chapter 15.)

Because the Israelis come from so many different lands, many different kinds of food are eaten in Israel. Families like Abraham's, from a Middle Eastern country, usually prefer the Arab dishes they ate in the old country. One Middle Eastern food, *felafel,** which is sold on the streets as a quick snack, is popular with almost everyone. Felafel is a garlic-flavored mixture of beans, peppers, and other vegetables, eaten as a sandwich filling.

Families like David's and Sarah's, from European countries, eat food more familiar to Western tastes. Some of their dishes are traditional Jewish ones also eaten by Jews in the United States. Gefilte* fish, a mixture of chopped fish, onions, eggs, and seasonings, is one of them. *Blintzes**, pancakes rolled up with a filling of cheese or fruit, is another. Many Jews are guided in their diet by strict rules based on Biblical

Behind the glitter of Israel's shop windows lies a quest for a better life for all Israelis. What does this Tel Aviv street scene reveal about the Israeli way of life?

laws. Their food is specially selected and prepared in order to be *kosher**, a word which comes from a Hebrew one meaning fit or proper.

Jews from many parts of the world are still coming to Israel. The Israelis call this immigration into the country *aliyah.** This is a word which means going up. The Isrealis think of the newcomers as people who are coming back to their true homeland.

Aliyah is a Hebrew word, and Hebrew is the language which David and Sarah speak. In Israel, schools teach Hebrew, radios broadcast in Hebrew, and newspapers are printed in and business carried on in Hebrew.

Like Israel itself, Hebrew is both old and new. Most of the Old Testament was originally written in Hebrew. But several centuries before the Romans drove them out of Palestine, Jews had already begun to use another Middle Eastern language, Aramaic.* Aramaic is the language Jesus spoke. Then during the 2,000 years they lived in other lands, the Jews spoke the languages of those lands. In Germany and Eastern European countries, they combined Hebrew words with German and other langauges to make up Yiddish. Many Jews throughout the world still speak Yiddish.

For all those years Jewish scholars and teachers and other students of the Bible and the Jewish religion continued to study Hebrew. Jewish religious services were conducted in it. For the most part, however, Hebrew was used just for prayer. No one used Hebrew as an everyday language until modern times. When Israel was founded, the Israelis made this old language the "new" language of their new country.

A modern language may contain hundreds or thousands of words. The ancient Hebrew of the Old Testament, however, contained only about 7,700 words. The Old Testament, of course, said nothing about radios, televisions, trains, jet planes, and all the other modern inventions and gadgets we take for granted.

To meet the demands of the modern world, Israeli scholars had to add countless new words to ancient Hebrew. Some words they borrowed from other languages—sports from English, for example. They also gave new meanings to some old Hebrew words. Hashmal,* for example, is used in the Bible to mean something which is bright or shining, or gives off light. Now the Israelis use hashmal to mean "electricity." *Gafrur** is the modern Hebrew word for a match. In the Bible, Gafrur was the brimstone rained down upon the cities of Sodom and Gomorrah for their sins.

THE HOLY LANDS

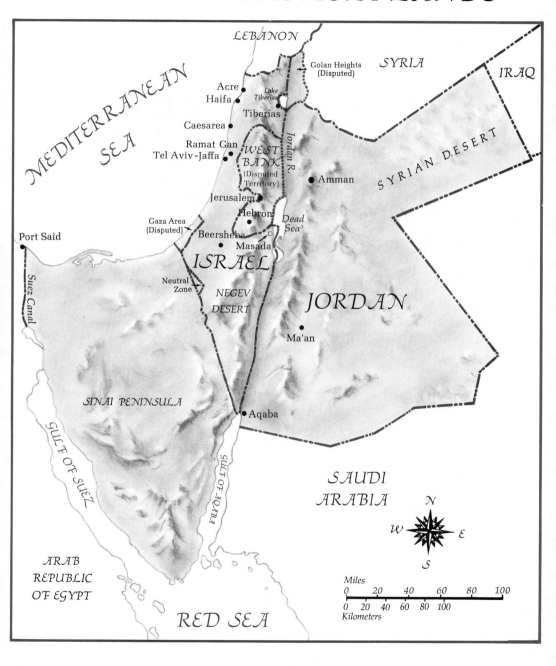

LEBANON

SYRIA

IRAQ

Golan Heights
(Disputed)

MEDITERRANEAN
SEA

Acre
Haifa

Lake
Tiberias

Tiberias

Caesarea

Ramat Gan
Tel Aviv-Jaffa

WEST
BANK
[Disputed
Territory]

Jordan R.

SYRIAN DESERT

Amman

Jerusalem

Hebron

Dead
Sea

Gaza Area
(Disputed)

Beersheba

Port Said

Masada

ISRAEL

JORDAN

Neutral
Zone

NEGEV
DESERT

Suez Canal

Ma'an

SINAI PENINSULA

Aqaba

GULF OF SUEZ

GULF OF AQABA

SAUDI
ARABIA

ARAB
REPUBLIC
OF EGYPT

N

W   E

S

RED SEA

Miles
0   20   40   60   80   100

0   20   40   60   80   100
Kilometers

Ancient mural, about 3,500 years old, shows enslaved Jews forced to carry heavy loads and lay bricks for Egyptians.

CENTURIES-OLD QUEST

THE ORIGINS OF the modern-day state of Israel go back about 4,000 years to Abraham, a shepherd who left his homeland in present-day Iraq in search of better pastureland. Eventually Abraham made his way into a land called Canaan.* Canaan was located roughly where Israel is today. Choosing a likely spot in this "Promised Land," Abraham set up his tents and dug seven wells. He named one of his new watering places Beersheba. (Beersheba still exists as a flourishing city. An ancient well there is said to be one that Abraham dug.)

But famine struck the new land, and Abraham's descendants left Canaan and migrated to Egypt. Four centuries later, Moses helped lead them back to Canaan.

It took the descendants of Abraham many years to gain control of the land of Canaan. Some two centuries passed before they were able to establish a kingdom there under kings such as David and Solomon. David made the city of Jerusalem his capital, and Solomon built a large temple there to house the Ark of the Covenant (the shrine which held the tablets on which were inscribed the Ten Commandments).

But eventually there was trouble. After Solomon's death, the kingdom split into two states — Israel in the north and Judah in the south. The people of Israel were carried off into slavery by the Assyrians. Years later, Judah was invaded by the Babylonians — who lived in what is now Iraq — and the temple in Jerusalem was destroyed. The Jews rebuilt it and, despite further invasions and conquests, they managed to keep their religion and their way of life alive.

Much later, the Romans took over Palestine. Unlike many other Roman subjects, the Jews refused to submit peacefully to Roman rule. They rose frequently in rebellion against the Romans. Finally the Romans burned Jerusalem and its temple to the ground.

Most of the Jews were driven from the land, although some did manage to stay. Most of those who were driven out settled in Europe or other parts of the Middle East. For centuries they were persecuted and discriminated against in their adopted countries. Often, they were forced to live in *ghettos** (special walled sections of cities). In Eastern Europe, they suffered *pogroms* — murderous attacks by their non-Jewish neighbors. The final horror came when the Nazi Germans slaughtered at least six million European Jews during World War II.

Through the centuries, however, the European Jews never forgot their ancient homeland. Their Passover prayer contained the hopeful phrase, *"Next year in Jerusalem."*

In the late 1800's, many Jews returned to Palestine, then controlled by the Ottoman Empire. After World War I, Britain took over Palestine, and more Jews began immigrating there. Their numbers were considerably expanded after World War II, when many survivors of Nazi concentration camps chose Palestine as their new home.

But the influx of Jews into Palestine stirred anger and resentment among the Arabs who lived there. To the Arabs, the Jews were strangers — people who had come from Europe to take land away from Arabs. Fighting broke out between Jews and Arabs. British troops, opposed by both sides, could not halt the violence. The British turned to the United Nations, which recommended that Palestine be split into separate Jewish and Arab states. The Arabs bitterly opposed the decision, but the Jews welcomed it. (During the fighting, many Arabs who were living in Palestine had become refugees. Many of these people and their children are still living in refugee camps in neighboring Arab countries. Their situation is a primary source of Arab-Israeli bitterness.)

On the afternoon of May 4, 1948, Jewish leaders gathered in a museum near Tel Aviv. There they proclaimed the birth of the state of Israel.

This was the signal for an all-out war to break out between Arabs and Israelis. It was ended by a truce, but three times more in the next quarter century (in 1956, 1967, and 1973) war broke out. Then in 1978, Egyptian President Anwar Sadat said that there had been too much killing. He visited Israel on a mission of peace. Several months later, in the United States, he and Israeli Prime Minister Menachim Begin signed a peace treaty.

Double-check

Review

1. In what year was Israel founded?

2. Almost all buildings in Israel are made of what materials?

3. When Israel was founded, what old language was made the "new" language of the new country?

4. Who helped lead the Jewish people out of Egypt into Canaan?

5. What were pogroms?

Discussion

1. Which of three Jewish immigrants to Israel — one from Boston, Moscow, or Fez — do you think would find living in Tel Aviv the most like living in his or her former city? Which immigrant would find the greatest differences between former and present cities? Why?

2. What problems do any people of differing backgrounds and cultures — such as those in Israel — confront in creating a new culture? How successful do you think the Israelis have been in developing a new culture? What problems have people of different cultural backgrounds faced upon arrival in the United States?

3. An Israeli law gives any Jew the right to settle in Israel. Why do you think this law was made? Should all people have a similar right to settle in the United States? If not, who should and who should not be allowed to settle here? Explain your answers.

Activities

1. A group of students might prepare a large timeline of the history of the Jewish people from the time of Abraham to the present.

2. Some students might look in the Bible for references to places that can be found in present-day Israel. The students could show the rest of the class where these places are located on a map of Israel.

3. Many books have been written about European pogroms and ghettos, Nazi concentration camps, and Jewish immigration to Palestine (later Israel). Some students might read one of these books (either fiction or nonfiction) and write a report on it to share with the class.

Skills

JEWISH HISTORY TIMELINE

c. 1750 B.C.

c. 1700–1600 B.C.

c. 1280 B.C.

930 B.C.

922 B.C.

586 B.C.

520–515 B.C.

70 A.D.

c. 1881 A.D.

1917 A.D.

1933–1945 A.D.

1948 A.D.

1967 A.D.

1978 A.D.

c. = approximately

A. Solomon dies.
B. Israel is founded.
C. Moses leads people to Canaan.
D. Jews suffer pogroms.
E. Abraham migrates to Canaan.
F. Temple in Jerusalem is rebuilt.
G. Kingdom is split into Judah and Israel.
H. Nazis kill six million Jews.
I. Romans burn Jerusalem and temple.
J. Egypt and Israel sign peace treaty.
K. Abraham's descendants go to Egypt.
L. Britain takes over Palestine.
M. Babylonians invade Judah.
N. Jews and Arabs fight Six Day War.

Chapter 13 describes each of the events listed above. The exact years in which some of the events took place are given in the chapter. For other events, figure out the years from other information in the chapter. For still other events, the only clue to their dates is the order in which they happened. Using the timeline above and by going back through the chapter, try to do the following on a separate sheet of paper.

1. Write the years given above down the left side of your paper.

2. Using the dates and the clues in the chapter, write the letter of each event next to the year in which it happened. (They are *not* in the correct order in the list above.)

Chapter 14

Farmers and Fighters

MANY ISRAELIS are newcomers, but one friend of David's and Sarah's parents, Nathan, has been living in Israel since 1925, when he came there from Poland as a young man. Nathan often tells the young people how in those days there was no country of Israel. The region was still know as Palestine, and Tel Aviv consisted of just a few houses along the shore. The Ottoman Empire had just ended. Palestine, which had been in the empire, was under British protection.

Nathan was a Zionist, which comes from the word Zion, the name used in the Bible for the hill in Jerusalem that 3,000 years ago was the site of the palace of King David. Zion was also used as a symbolic name for Jerusalem and the land of Israel.

The Zionists were members of an organization which had been formed in Europe around 1900. They recalled that Palestine had been the ancient homeland of the Jews and that, in the Bible, God had promised the land of Israel to Abraham and his descendents. This is why Israel is often called the Promised Land. In 1925 the people living in Palestine were mostly Arabs. But Zionists had begun to settle there as early as the 1880's and to work toward the founding of their own country. This finally happened in 1948. That year, the United Nations decided that a large part of Palestine should become a Jewish nation called Israel.

Newcomers to Israel now started attending Hebrew schools as soon as they arrive in the country. For older people, it's sometimes very hard. Abraham's parents knew only Arabic, the major language of Morocco. It took them a long time to learn Hebrew. *Sabras** such as David and Sarah are fortunate; they grew up speaking Hebrew. The sabra is a cactus plant that grows in Israel, and the Israelis use the word to mean people born there. Young Israelis are like sabras, they say, tough on the outside, like the plant's prickly skin, but sweet, like its fruit, on the inside.

David and Sarah both attend classes six days a week. Their holiday is Saturday, the Jewish holy day. They study geography, history, mathematics, and science, and they must learn English as well as Hebrew. In high school, students may study a third language if they wish, usually French or Arabic.

Both David and Sarah study the Hebrew Bible in class. In Israel it is used as a textbook because it tells the history of the Jewish people.

The Jews were the first people to develop a lasting religion based on *monotheism.** This word comes from two Greek ones, monos, "one," and theos, "god," and means belief in One God. Many of the great religions today are monotheistic. When the Jews first expressed the idea, it was new.

The famous words expressing this idea are contained

190

About 1900 many Jews began emigrating to Palestine with the hope of some day making it a Jewish state. It took special pride to create the nation of Israel, the kind of pride illustrated in this photo of a Jewish clean-up crew in 1935.

in a single sentence from the Book of Deuteronomy.* Deuteronomy is one of the first five books of the Torah*, or Jewish law. It is also part of the Old Testament used by Christians. In it, Moses, the great leader of the Jews, calls upon his people to remember God's teach-

191

ings: "Hear, O Israel, the Lord our God, the Lord is One." These are words which many pious Jews repeat everyday in their morning and evening prayers.

Two other major religions, Islam and Christianity, have adopted the monotheism first developed by Judiasm. Moslems are expressing their montheism when the muezzins call people to prayer five times a day. They always begin with the words: "There is no God but Allah, and Mohammed is his Messenger."

Many Christians learn it in this translation of the words of the first of the Ten Commandments: "I am the Lord thy God...Thou shalt have no other gods before me."

Many Israeli young people spend some of their free learning farming and other kinds of outdoor work. Most do not plan to be farmers, but they like to feel that they are helping their country. On long holidays David, who belongs to the Israeli Boy Scouts, spends several days with his troop helping out on a special kind of Israeli farm called a *kibbutz**.

A kibbutz tries to provide everything its people need to live—food, clothing, housing, schools, and medical care. Not all the kibbutz members are farmers. Some are cooks. Some are teachers. Some work in the laundry or the clinic. Some take care of 10 small children while their parents are in the fields.

The first kibbutz farms—or kibbutzim—were set up about 1910. Later, after the country of Israel was established, the Jewish settlers banded together to form many more of them. So much had to be done to make the land good for farming—like draining the swamps and irrigating dry areas—that settlers decided the best

Work on the kibbutz is often difficult — and sometimes dangerous. This Israeli teenager keeps one hand on the steering wheel of his tractor and the other hand near his rifle.

"The soil is good and we are using it to grow things. None of us will be rich here, but we will be comfortable."

way to do it was to work together.

There are hundreds of kibbutzim in Israel today. Some Israelis prefer this kind of life to any other, especially sabras who were born on a kibbutz. Rafi is 22 and a worker on an Israeli kibbutz. Rafi's kibbutz is located in territory that was controlled by Syria until it was captured by Israel in the 1967 war.

Two years ago, when Rafi was in the Israeli army, he worked in the special corps which builds fortified farming settlements on Israel's borders as a form of defense. The experience convinced him that farming was what he wanted for his life. After finishing his army service, he and three friends volunteered to start a settlement in the newly occupied areas.

Today 23 young men and women work at this settlement. With government financial help and advice, they are raising experimental crops, trying to discover what grows best in the area.

Rafi's group works long, hard hours. They are in the fields before dawn and work until dusk. In the evenings they discuss the next day's work, then visit, or watch television. They have little time for outside social life.

"The soil is good and we are using it to grow things," Rafi says. "None of us will be rich here, but we will be comfortable."

In three years, when David is 18 and has finished high school, he will join the army, just as Rafi did. In Israel, everyone—even girls if they are unmarried—must spend some time in the army. For boys, it's usually three years. For girls it's a little less. Sarah thinks this will be exciting.

In 73 A.D. the hilltop outpost of Masada was the site of a heroic last stand by 960 Jews against the mighty Roman army.

MASADA:
FORTRESS OF FREEDOM

IN THE FIRST CENTURY A.D., the area which is now Israel was under Roman rule. Then, in 66 A.D., the Jews revolted. The uprising was crushed, but one lone outpost — Masada* — held out. There 960 men, women, and children resisted the mighty Roman armies for three long years. In the end, they chose death rather than surrender and slavery.

The story of Masada is best known through the writings of one historian of that time: Josephus, a Jew who worked with the Romans. According to his reports, Roman armies built a ramp to the top of the cliff on which Masada stood and attacked the fort with a battering ram and flaming missiles. As the Romans got closer, Eleazar ben Yair,* the commander of the garrison, called his people together. Defeat, he told them, was certain. By dawn the Romans would take the garrison.

But, proposed the commander, there was an alternative to capture. Let us burn our possessions, slay our wives and children. Then let us draw lots, select some from among us to kill the rest. This, wrote Josephus, was what they did. Next day, as the triumphant Romans came dashing through the breach in the wall, they were met only by smoldering ruins and silence — a silence that signified the final defiance.

Josephus was not at Masada at the time of the battle. He got his information through the only survivors of Masada — two elderly women and several children who had hidden in an old well rather than be killed.

But how do we know whether the survivors were telling the truth — and whether Josephus reported accurately? What evidence is there to back up his story? Until recently there was none — and no one really knew whether the story of Masada was fact or fiction.

But a few years ago, an expedition made a careful study of Masada. It dug down through some 2,000 years and several layers of history to uncover the original buildings. The expedition's findings seemed to confirm Josephus' history of the fall of Masada. For example, Josephus had written that the men, after killing their own families, "not being able to bear the grief they were under for what they had done any longer,... laid out all they had in a heap and set fire to it." The diggers, almost 2,000 years later, found small piles of ashes in the rooms used by the defenders of Masada. Among them were the charred remains of children's sandals, water jars, and other household items.

"They then," according to Josephus, "chose 11 men by lot...to slay all the rest,...and when these 11 had, without fear, slain them all, they made the same rule for casting lots for themselves, that he whose lot it was should first kill the other 10 and, after all, should kill himself." This is backed up by what is perhaps the expedition's most dramatic discovery. In one of the rooms of the fortress, diggers found 11 small, broken-off pieces of pottery, each inscribed in Hebrew with a name. One of the names was "Ben Ya'ir," commander of the garrison.

Of the man chosen in the lottery to be the last to die, Josephus wrote: "And he who was last of all took a view of the other bodies...and when he perceived that they were all slain, he set fire to the palace, and with the force of his hand ran his sword entirely through himself." All the buildings excavated were coated with a thick layer of ashes, evidence of a massive fire.

Piece of pottery, bearing Hebrew letters for Ben Ya'ir, was unearthed at Masada. Ben Ya'ir was commander of Jewish forces at Masada.

Double-check

Review

1. Who are Zionists?

2. Which day of the week is Sarah's holiday?

3. What is a kibbutz?

4. The men, women, and children at Masada resisted what armies for three years?

5. How did Josephus get his information about Masada?

Discussion

1. Before 1967 about 15 per cent of Israel's gross national product was spent on the military. In the late 1970's, 30 per cent of the GNP went to military expenses. Why do you suppose the percentage doubled? Do you think the increase was justified? How much of a country's wealth should be spent on the military? On what factors might your answer depend?

2. In Israeli public schools, the Old Testament is commonly used as a textbook. In the United States, religious books are rarely used in public schools. Why is there this difference between the school systems of Israel and the United States?

3. When people join a kibbutz in Israel, they have to give up most of their wealth and valuables to the kibbutz. Property is owned in common by all members. Members do not receive a salary. Instead the kibbutz takes care of the needs of its members. Do you think this is a good system? Why, or why not?

Activities

1. A group of students might interview a person who has visited or lived in Israel. Ask the interviewee to describe life on a kibbutz, urban life, military service, and school life in Israel. Each interviewer could take notes and write a brief report about the interview.

2. A committee of students might plan and prepare a bulletin board display titled "Farming in Israel." They could collect pictures and articles about modern methods of farming, types of farms, irrigation of the desert, and social life on Israeli farms.

3. Other students might research and draw two maps: (a) the British-controlled nation of Palestine; (b) the nation of Israel that was created in 1948.

Skills

EDUCATION IN THE MIDDLE EAST, 1981

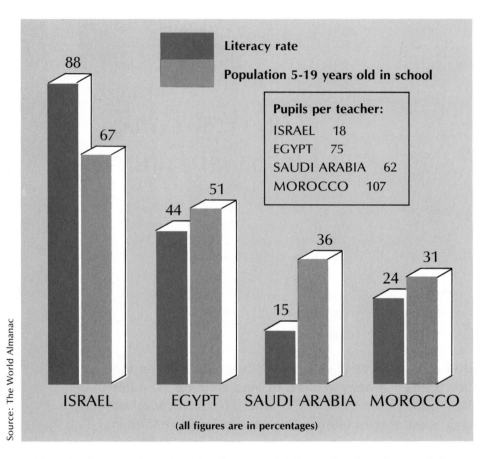

Legend:
- Literacy rate
- Population 5-19 years old in school

Pupils per teacher:
ISRAEL 18
EGYPT 75
SAUDI ARABIA 62
MOROCCO 107

Bar values:
ISRAEL 88, 67
EGYPT 44, 51
SAUDI ARABIA 15, 36
MOROCCO 24, 31

ISRAEL EGYPT SAUDI ARABIA MOROCCO

(all figures are in percentages)

Source: The World Almanac

Use the bar graph and table above and information in Chapter 14 to answer the following questions.

1. What do the light bars show? What do the dark bars show?

2. What do the numbers in the boxed table represent?

3. What percentage of Egypt's population was literate in 1981?

4. Judging from the bar graph, is it true that the higher the percentage of a nation's population aged 5 to 19 that is in school, the higher the literacy rate of the nation will be?

5. In which of the four countries listed above would you expect to find the fewest students per classroom?

Chapter 15

The West Bank: Uncertain Future

MOSHE IS A 12-YEAR-OLD Israeli boy who lives on the West Bank—a narrow piece of land running 70 miles along the western bank of the Jordan River. In Moshe's town, most of the buildings are new. In fact, the town is only 10 years old. It is one of the more than 100 Jewish settlements set up on the West Bank since Israel occupied the area in 1967.

Amina, a 13-year old Palestinian Arab girl, also lives on the West Bank in a centuries-old Arab town. Although she's only 15 minutes away from Moshe by car, the two might as well live in different worlds.

Moshe and Amina are caught in the middle of a political storm. The West Bank, an area rich in history, is disputed territory. Israeli settlers claim it as part of their ancient homeland. They call the West Bank by its Biblical name: Samaria. The Palestinians, who have lived here for centuries, want the West Bank to be an independent Arab state.

The conflict dates back to the creation of Israel in 1948. At that time, the United Nations divided Palestine into two areas: one for Arabs and the other for Jews. The West Bank was the heart of the Arab area.

It was expected that both areas would become independent nations. The Jewish area did become the nation of Israel. But the Arabs refused to accept the U.N. division of Palestine or recognize the existence of Israel. They thought all of Palestine should belong to the Arabs who lived there.

Arabs of other nations agreed with the Palestinian Arabs. Theydeclared war on the infant state of Israel. During that war, 700,000 Arabs living in Palestine left their homes. Why they did so is disputed. Arabs claim that the Israelis chased them out. The Israelis say that the Arab armies encouraged civilians to leave until the final destruction of Israel was accomplished.

By the time the war ended in January 1949, Israel had survived attacks by six Arab armies. It held more territory than it had been granted under the U.N. plan. The rest of Palestine was in the hands of Arab nations: Syria, Egypt and Jordan. Jordan controlled the West Bank.

Palestinian refugees lived in all these Arab nations. In some areas, such as the West Bank, they mixed in with the people already living there. However, many refugees who had fled out of Palestine completely, into the neighboring Arab countries, were forced to live in refugee camps. This kept them in poverty and sometimes squalor. The Palestinian state envisioned by the U.N. never came to be.

War broke out between Israel and its Arab neighbors in 1956 and in 1967. In the later war, which lasted only six days, Israel made a massive and successful effort to come back from near destruction. War's end left the Israelis in possession of all of Palestine including the West Bank. In 1973, Arab armies invaded once more. But they failed to regain what they had lost seven years before.

Israeli settlement of the West Bank began in earnest after the 1973 war. Those who moved to the area came for a variety of motives. Some were attracted by the low cost of housing. Many sections of the West Bank are an easy commute from Jerusalem and other Israeli cities.

But many more Israeli settlers came out of conviction. A large part of the ancient, Biblical history of the Jewish people took place on the West Bank. Settlers believe they are returning to their heritage by living there. They also see themselves as exerting an historic right that Jews have to the area.

Arabs have lashed out at the Israeli government for allowing, indeed encouraging, Jewish settlement of the West Bank. They accuse Israel of preparing to annex the area—make it a formal part of Israel. The vast majority of Palestinians want the West Bank to be the independent homeland they have never had. Some Palestinians, frustrated by their powerlessness to change the situation, have turned to terrorism.

The Palestinian Liberation Organization (P.L.O.) is a well-known terrorist group. On the West Bank, there is some organized terrorism, but also much random violence. Jewish settlers are gunned down, buses hijacked, and buildings burned. The Israeli army which patrols the West Bank tries to stamp out this violence. However the army's actions, according to many Arabs, are just as bad as the terrorists'. The army has been ac-

These Palestinian refugees have lost their homes and now live in crowded refugee camps.

⮎ Many Palestinians are forced to live in refugee camps.

cused of torturing suspects, destroying property, and humiliating law-abiding citizens.

This is the situation in which Moshe and Amina live. Both have escaped personal experience with violence, but they know about the realities around them.

When Moshe or his family travel outside their town they often go in groups. When they do leave—to work or to shop—many people carry guns in their cars for protection. On a recent school trip, three armed guards accompanied Moshe's class.

"Having these experiences is part of living here, I don't think about it every day," Moshe says. He's proud to be living where he does, "where Jewish history really began."

When Amina's father drives her to school they are stopped at the Israeli military post less than a mile from their home. Sometimes their car is inspected. Other times, the soldiers just want to see their identity papers. Amina has often seen men forced to stand with their hands against a wall while they are searched.

Amina is adamant on the subject of the future of the West Bank. "The Israeli settlers on the West Bank should go back to where they came from."

She hopes that by the time she grows up, the Palestinian issue will be settled. "I want to raise my children where it is not illegal to raise the Palestinian flag."

But Amina's dream may not come true. The conflict over the West Bank already 20 years old, and has no easy solution in view. It is a land that two peoples claim as their own.

Only in a few places, such as the city of Jerusalem (right), do Arabs and Jews actually meet to discuss their differences. As the raised eyebrows and drawn faces of these two men indicate, they have a lot more talking to do before their differences can be solved. After reading this book, do you think their differences can be solved peacefully?

204

Double-check

Review

1. What two peoples claim the West Bank as their own?

2. How did the U.N. divide Palestine in 1948?

3. Why did many Palestinians refuse to accept the U.N. settlement?

4. For what two reasons might Israeli Jews live on the West Bank?

5. What dreams do Palestinians have for the West Bank?

Discussion

1. Based on what you read in this chapter, have you come to any conclusions about the future of the West Bank? How might both the Israelis and the Palestinians be satisfied?

2. Put yourself in the shoes of a Israeli leader. Would you encourage or discourage further Jewish settlement on the West Bank? Before answering consider all the interests of the people you are leading. How will Israeli security be affected by further settlement? What about relations with other Arab nations?

3. Why do you think some Palestinians have turned to terrorism to make their grievances known to the world? Is terrorism ever justifiable? Explain your answer.

Activities

1. Have a class debate on the future of the West Bank. The class should be divided into two groups. One group might prepare to present the point of view of Israeli settlers who want the area to become part of Israel. The other group could represent Palestinians who dream of an independent homeland on the West Bank. Students may want to consult newspapers, magazines, and other books to prepare their positions.

2. Have students scan newspapers daily to keep track of what's happening on the West Bank. They should prepare to update the class on such topics as new Israeli settlements, terrorist incidents, army brutality, and international agreements pertaining to the West Bank.

THREE COUNTRIES' ARMED FORCES PERSONNEL
1979-1983

Numbers in thousands

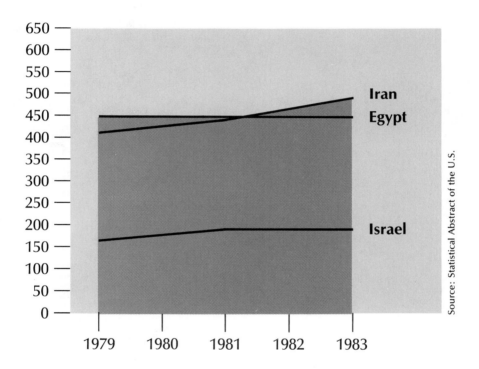

Source: Statistical Abstract of the U.S.

Use the line graph above and information in chapters 13, 14, and 15 to answer the following questions.

1. What do the numbers on the left of the graph represent? How many years does the information no this graph cover?

2. What country's armed forces stayed exactly the same size between 1979-1983?

3. How many members of the armed forces did Iran have in 1979?

4. The Iranian revolution occurred in 1979. Since then has the size of Iran's armed forces increased or decreased?

EPILOGUE

A LOOK AHEAD, A LOOK BEHIND

THE STRUGGLE between Arabs and Israelis and the Islamic reawakening make headlines almost every day. The daily life of Middle Easterners is rarely news. Yet, as we have seen, there is much more to life in the Middle East than stories which make headlines. True, the Arab-Israeli dispute and the Islamic renewal are close for some Middle Easterners, but not for all.

It would be a mistake to think that all of the people of Israel live one way of life, and all of the people of the Moslem countries another. Despite the divisions of religion and politics, there is no rigid line between the two peoples. Before 1979, Yasmine, in Teheran, would have had more in common with David in Tel Aviv than with Hassan in his "house of hair" in the Arabian desert. Avraham's father, who came to Israel from Fez in Morocco, might feel more at home with Khaled's father, who lives in Fez, than with David's father who came to Israel from Poland by way of Britain.

Obviously, all Israelis are not alike. Some are religious and some aren't. Some have their roots in the Arab Middle East; some, in Eastern Europe; and some, in Western Europe and the U.S.

If this diversity is true for Israel, it is even truer for the Arab lands. Depending on where they live and how they earn their living, Arab peoples follow ways of life that are sharply different from one another. Kuwaitis, for example, are mostly business people or government workers. Most Egyptians, except for those who live in the large cities, are farmers, tilling the land in almost the same manner as their ancient ancestors. And the Bedouins of the Arabian and Saharan deserts know little of either farming or business.

While the Arab and Ottoman empires were at their heights, most of the Arab and Moslem countries were united under a single ruler. Now that is changed. There are many independent countries with many different kinds of governments. A few are republics; there the people elect their government officials democratically. Many others have far less democracy, or

❧ Almost everyone's life is changing, sometimes rapidly, usually slowly — but changing nevertheless.

Egyptian fellahin inspect model of a U.S. space capsule.

none at all. They may be called republics, but one man or a small group of men have all the real power. Others are monarchies ruled by a king, sultan, sheik, or emir. He may, or may not, share some of his power with his people.

All of these differences have led to disagreements at times. In recent years many of the Arab countries have had serious quarrels with one another. Often the Arab republics have been at bitter odds with the Arab monarchies. But these divisions are not new. Throughout the centuries, the peoples of the deserts, the farmlands, and the towns have not mixed well together. The Bedouins have generally considered themselves better than the fellahin and the city Arabs. Until modern times the settled people have feared the tough and warlike desert tribesmen.

Yet the Arab countries maintain a bond which no differences seem able to break. These countries have a common culture, and this is one of the strongest ties that can bind people together.

Culture is a term that is often used, but little understood. What does it mean? It includes people's customs, the way they look at life and the world, the beliefs that they hold, their language, the way they express themselves in art and literature. Almost all the people of the Middle East are Moslems, and their attitudes, their arts, and their customs almost all stem from Islam.

The way Middle Easterners build their houses, for example, differs only slightly from country to country. Most houses — even "houses of hair" — have one thing in common: they have been designed to keep the lives of women as private as possible, and to shield the family from the eyes of strangers. Outside the large cities, loyalty to one's clan or tribe is one of the most important things in life. In some places, as in the Arabian desert, it is often more important than loyalty to government.

Most Middle Easterners speak the same language, Arabic. The kind of "every-day" Arabic which Munir and Ali speak in Cairo is quite different from that which Khaled speaks in Fez. In fact, Munir and Ali would have a hard time holding a conversation with Khaled. But the "formal" Arabic in which all three pray — the old, "classical" Arabic in which the Koran is written — is the same. The Koran binds the three young people together. So does the Arab past, with all the Arab works of poetry, philosophy, and science which were written in the language of the Koran.

The Islamic cultural bond is one of the most important things about the Middle East. But another is the change which is now taking place in all of them. Almost everyone's life is changing, sometimes rapidly, usually slowly — but changing nevertheless.

In some countries, the change is toward Westernization. There is something new almost everywhere. Even a single transistor radio in a remote Arab village, even a truck on the horizon of a desert where once only Bedouins and camels walked, makes a difference.

In other countries, the trend toward Westernization has been challenged by a renewed interest in traditional Islamic laws and customs.

It is still unclear how these conflicting trends will affect the countries — and the people — of the Middle East in the coming decades. But it does seem clear that whatever happens will be interesting and will have great impact on the rest of the world.

Pronunciation Guide

The following system translates each syllable into the nearest common English equivalent. Syllables set in capitals are accented. Principal sound equivalents are:

a (as in cat)
ah (as in odd)
aw (as in lawn)
ay (as in ale)
e (as in silent)
ee (as in eat)
eh (as in end)
g (as in go)
i (as in charity)
ie (as in ice)
ih (as in ill)
j (as in John)
k (as in keep)
o (as in connect)

oe (as in hoe)
oh (as in old)
oo (as in too)
or (as in for)
ow (as in out)
s (as in sit)
sh (as in ship)
t (as in tin)
th (as in then)
u (as in circus)
uh (unaccented a as in sofa)
ur (as in urn)
y (as in yet)
z (as in zebra)

Abdullah — ahb-DUHL-uh
abla — AH-bluh
Acre — AY-kur
Ahmed — AH-mehd
al-Azhar — ahl-AHZ-hahr
aliyah — ah-lee-YAH
Amina — uh-MEE-nuh
Aramaic — ar-uh-MAY-ihk
Ararat — A-ruh-rat
Aswan — ahs-WAHN
Ataturk — AT-uh-turk
Ayatollah Ruhollah Khomeini — ïe-ah-TOHL-luh
    roo-HOHL-luh hoe-MAY-nee

Babylonians — bab-uh-LOH-ny-uhnz
Baghdad — BAG-dad
Bashar — buh-SHAHR
Bedouin — BEHD-uh-wuhn
Beersheba — beer-SHEE-buh
blintzes — BLIHNT-sihz
Bosporus — BOS-puh-ruhs
Byzantine — BIHZ-'n-teen

Caesarea — seh-suh-REE-uh
Cairo — KIE-roh
caliph — kah-LEEF
Canaan — KAY-nuhn
cuneiform — kyoo-NEE-uh-fohrm

Damascus — duh-MAS-kuhs
Dardanelles — dahr-duh-NEHLZ
Deuteronomy — dyoo-tuh-RAHN-uh-mee

efendim — eh-FEHN-dihm
Eleazar ben Yair — ehl-yuh-ZAHR behn yah-EER
emir — ih-MIHR
Ephesus — EH-fuh-suhs
Euphrates — yoo-FRAY-teez

Fatimah — FAH-tee-muh
Fawzia — fow-ZEE-yuh
felafel — f'-LAH-fuhl

fellahin — FEHL-luh-heen
Fouad — FOO-ad

gafrur — guh-FROOR
Gamal Abdel Nasser — guh-MAHL AHB-d'l NAHS-uhr
gefilte — guh-FIHL-tuh
ghettos — GEH-tohz
Gibraltar — jih-BRAHL-tuhr

Habimah — hah-BEE-muh
Haifa — HIE-fah
Hakan — HAH-kahn
Hamid — HAH-mihd
harem — HAR-uhm
Haroun — hah-ROON
Hashem — HAH-shehm
hashmal — hahsh-MAHL
Hasidic — hah-SEE-dihk
Hassan — HAH-suhn
Hawalli — huh-WAH-lee
Hebron — HEE-bruhn
hegira — HEH-gee-rah
hora — HOH-ruh

Istanbul — ihs-tan-BOOL

Jaffa — JAH-fuh

kebab—keh-BAB
keffiyah—KEHF-ee-yuh
Khadija—Khuh-DEE-jhuh
Khaled—KHAH-lehd
kibbutz—kihb-OOTS
Koran—KOH-ran
kosher—KOH-shuhr

Mahmud — MAH-mood
mahr — MEH-hehr
Marmara —- MAHR-muh-ruh
Masada — muh-SAH-duh
medina, Medina — muh-DEE-nuh
Menes — MEE-neez
minaret — mihn-uh-REHT

monotheism — MAH-nuh-thee-ihz-uhm
mosque — MAHSK
muezzin — MWEHZ-'n
Munir — moo-NEER
Murrah — MOOR-uh
Mustafa Kemal — MOOS-tuh-fuh KEH-mahl

Najeba — na-JEE-bah

oasis — oh-AY-suhs
Omar — OH-mahr

pharaoh — FEH-roh

Ramadan — RAH-muh-dahn
Ramat Gan — ruh-MAHT GAHN
Riyadh — ree-YAHD

sabras — SAH-bruhs
Safiya — sah-FEE-yuh
Salamah — suh-LAH-muh
shadoof — shuh-DOOF
Shah Mohammed Riza Pahlevi — shaw mo-HAH-mud
  REE-zuh pah-LAH-vee
sheik — SHEEK
Sinai — SIGH-nigh
Suleiman — SOO-lay-mahn
Sumerians — soo-MEH-ree-uhnz
Syed — SY-ihd

Teheran — TEH-huh-RAN
Tel Aviv — TEHL ah-VEEV
Tiberias — tigh-BEE-ree-uhs
Tigris — TIGH-grihs
Topkapi — TOP-kuh-puh
Torah — TOH-ruh
Tugsavul — TOO-suh-vool

Yasmine — yas-MEEN

Zeynep — ZAY-nehp
zurkhaneh — zer-KAH-neh
Zvi — ts'-VEE

Index

*Photograph